CUBS AT PLAY

Stephen Andrews

Illustrated by Val Biro

Beaver Books

A Beaver Book

Published by Arrow Books Limited
17-21 Conway Street, London W1P 6JD

An imprint of the Hutchinson Publishing Group

London Melbourne Sydney Auckland
Johannesburg and agencies throughout
the world

First published by Hodder & Stoughton 1977
Beaver edition 1986

Printed and bound in Great Britain by
Anchor Brendon Limited, Tiptree, Essex

ISBN 0 09 943440 7

Contents

1 · Scratch team

AKELA looked across the Cub hall at the four dark windows in the wall.

'Draw the curtains, Snowy,' he said. 'Let's keep in the heat.'

'Snowy' White, the Tawny Brown Sixer, drew the curtains across the cold, dark panes. The hall felt a little cosier for the thirty-six Cub Scouts gathered there for their weekly Friday meeting.

'We've had some good outings this summer,' went on Akela. 'Now the nights are drawing in, and the cold weather is almost on us.'

The Cubs groaned.

'Don't look so miserable,' said Akela. 'We don't have to be glum for the next six months. Just think of all the winter sports we can play. There's football, swimming, running . . .'

'Nobby' Clark, the Tawny Brown Second, put up his hand. 'Snowball fights!' he said.

Akela frowned. 'Yes . . . if you like snowball fights and you have some snow. And if you have the snow, you can go sledging. But you don't need snow for winter sports. I . . . I remember I used to do my boating right up to Christmas. What I'm trying to say is that we can enjoy a winter season as much as we enjoyed the summer season.'

Akela paced the floor to collect his thoughts.

'The football season starts in three weeks,' he said. 'Last night I telephoned West Park Cub Scouts and challenged them to a football match. What do you think of that?'

'Football?' said Nobby.

'Yes, football!' said Akela. 'Football is a sport, and sport is part of Scouting.'

'We . . . we haven't got a football team,' said Snowy.

'We'll get one!' Akela grinned. 'Listen, we've got three weeks before the football season starts. We can get in a lot of practice before then on that field just behind here. Don't look so glum. It doesn't really matter if we win or lose.'

'We'll win all right,' chirped up Nobby. 'I reckon we'll beat West Park seventy-two–nil.'

'Seventy-two–nil?' echoed Akela.

'Yes,' chirped Nobby. 'We'll be in the Book of Records as the world's greatest winners.'

'If the 2nd Billingtons end up in the Book of Records,' scoffed Akela, 'I'll buy you all a round of fish and chips.'

'With salt and vinegar on mine, please,' said Nobby.

Thirty-six Cubs turned up the next morning for their first football practice match on the patch of spare ground behind Group Headquarters. The result can only be described as a comic show.

When Snowy got the ball, he found he had no one to pass it to. Everyone on the field, with the exception of the goalkeepers, charged after him like a pack of hounds. Snowy exhausted himself by dribbling the ball down the field and was almost trampled under the feet of the following mob. In less than fifteen minutes after kick-off, every player, with the exception of the goalkeepers, was exhausted, and could not run another step.

Only the goalkeepers had the energy to carry on the game, and they did. Nobby Clark, who was playing goalkeeper for the whites, scored for his team. Akela threw his beret in a puddle and jumped on it.

'Do we look as bad as we are?' gasped Snowy.

'Worse!' said Akela in despair. 'Worse than worse.'

'Never mind,' said Nobby. 'We'll show West Park. I reckon we'll beat them about fifty-three–nil.'

'I reckon they'll beat us fifty-three–nil,' wailed Akela. 'I made a big mistake when I challenged West Park. I should have stuck to tiddley-winks!'

But gradually the Cubs, under Akela's coaching, settled down. They saw how useless it was to charge all over the field after the ball. They learnt to gain ground by passing the ball from player to player. Best of all, Akela taught them tactics. The 2nd Billington Cub Scout football team improved – slowly.

On the morning of the great match, the Scouts were raising money to buy an old canal barge, by washing down cars at Group Headquarters for twenty-five pence a time. Some of the Cubs volunteered to help, trying not to be too tense about the match they were due to play in the afternoon.

Then a bus arrived. Nobby looked up from a car he was polishing.

'Do you want that big thing cleaning?' he gasped. 'It . . . it will take six months to clean all that.'

The bus-driver looked out of his cab.

'Is this the 2nd Billington Cub Scout Pack?' he asked.

'Yes,' said Snowy. 'That's us.'

'I've come to collect the football team.'

'But our match isn't until this afternoon,' said Snowy.

'What's up, driver?' said Akela, coming across to see what the trouble was.

'I've come for the football team. I've got to take them to South Lancs Playing Fields by half-past ten. Pitch number seventeen.'

'Pitch seventeen?' said Akela. 'That's right, but we're not due to play until this afternoon.'

'Not by my time-table,' said the bus-driver, waving his job sheet. 'There's a junior match on pitch seventeen this afternoon, Trafford Juniors against Stanley Town Juniors. First round of the All-England Junior Cup. I have to pick up the Trafford lads for their match this afternoon.'

Akela scratched his head. 'There must be some mistake. We're playing West Park at South Lancs Playing Fields this afternoon, on pitch seventeen.'

The bus-driver looked at his job sheet. 'Look, mister, are you coming or aren't you? I've got a girl's hockey team to pick up at eleven. I can't waste time.

If I'm late now, I'll be late all through the day.'

Akela looked at the bus-driver's job sheet. 'Looks as if you're right!'

'I know I'm right. Haven't you seen the posters all over town – Trafford Juniors versus Stanley Town Juniors this afternoon? There'll be dozens of spectators there this afternoon, and I don't think they'll be turning up for you.'

'Well, they'd better not see us,' said Akela. 'Now you go back without us, and give West Park my apologies. Tell them, as soon as I round up my team, I'll be there in our mini-bus.'

The bus-driver slammed his gear-stick in reverse.

'O.K., I'll tell them that. Can I reverse straight out?'

'Yes, there's a Scout on the gate who'll back you out. Sorry to have troubled you.'

'No trouble to me, mate. I just do my job.'

The bus-driver let out his clutch as a Scout waved him back. Akela turned to his Cubs.

'Snowy! Nobby! Dash home and pick up your football kit. Give Bobbie and Louie a shout on the way. Tell them the match has been brought forward. I'll pick you up at the corner in the mini-bus.'

'What about the others?' asked Snowy.

'I'll see to them. You go off as sharp as you can, but watch the traffic. What did I say?'

'Watch the traffic!' repeated Snowy.

'Right!' Akela dashed off to the Scout mini-bus.

'We'd better get our skates on,' said Snowy, giving Nobby a nudge.

'I didn't know we were going skating!' said Nobby.

'Ah, come on!'

Akela picked up all his team within twelve minutes, and to save time, the Cubs changed into their red football shirts in the mini-bus. They arrived at the playing fields only five minutes late.

The South Lancs Playing Fields stretched almost as far as the eye could see. Separate games were being played all over. Young players sported shirts of all colours. Most were playing football, but some were playing rugby and some hockey. There was even a late game of cricket being played in front of the pavilion.

Akela drove the mini-bus as near to pitch number seventeen as he could. Already warming up on the pitch, were the Cubs' opponents, in their striking purple and blue shirts.

The purple and blue shirted players flicked the ball to one another with uncanny grace, encouraged by a trainer wearing a professional footballer's track suit. Occasionally, one of the players would shoot the ball goalwards like a cannon-ball. These boys were fast. They were strong. The 2nd Billington Cubs had improved their play over the past three weeks, but here, they were obviously out of their class.

Akela walked across to the opposing trainer and shook hands. Snowy led his team on to the field. He could not recognise any of the West Park players. However, one of their players, a lad who moved like a bunch of coiled springs, smiled at him.

'Hi,' he said. 'My name's Chunky – well, that's what they call me, Chunky Craig.'

'Sorry we're late,' said Snowy. 'We had a mix-up with the times.'

'That's all right. We don't mind waiting if you want to warm up. First meet the boys. Mike, Walter our best striker, Chris Sharples the goalkeeper, Ron, Charlie, sweeper . . .'

Chunky went on to introduce his team. Snowy did likewise, all the time feeling he was up against powerful opposition. Snowy found it difficult not to be down-hearted. He could not see, for the life of him, how he could even give his opponents a decent game.

The opposing trainer blew his whistle and ran on to the pitch waving his arms. Akela came after him with his head bowed.

'Game's off, game's off!' said the trainer as his players gathered round him. 'Our match is this afternoon, not this morning. Two o'clock this afternoon, against Trafford Juniors.'

Akela came across to his Cubs. 'What a mix-up!' he said, shaking his head. 'These aren't West Park

Cubs. They're ... they're Stanley Town Juniors.'

'Who's Stanley Town?' asked Nobby.

Akela shrieked. 'Stanley Town was one of the first teams in the Football League. They've been League Champions goodness knows how many times. The place still has a reputation for football. These juniors are one of the best teams in the country. They're all up-and-coming professional footballers. Their trainer over there, is Matt Wilson, an ex-Welsh International. If we played these boys, the score would be ... oh ... oh ... a thousand–nil!'

'That's a bit high,' said Nobby.

'No, it's not! It's definitely not!'

'I don't think we could score a thousand—'

'Not you, them!' wailed Akela, nearly tearing out his hair.

'Sorry about the mix-up,' said the trainer, coming up to Akela. 'Our match is this afternoon.'

'We can still give you a game,' suggested Chunky.

'No, no, no, no,' said his trainer, firmly. 'We've got a very important match this afternoon, and I don't want any of you to risk getting hurt. No, no, no. Another time, gladly, when we're free. Not now. No, no. Not today. No.'

Akela heaved a sigh of relief. 'Back to the mini-bus, Cubs,' he said. He turned to the trainer. 'To be honest,' he said, 'we couldn't give you a decent game. We're nowhere near your class. Cricket, yes, football, no . . .'

'We'll give you a game of cricket then,' spoke up Chunky. 'If that's all right with you, trainer?'

The trainer shrugged his shoulders. 'We have no cricket gear . . .'

'We've got a set in the boot,' said Akela, 'unless somebody borrowed it without telling me.'

'Well, twenty-five overs each way won't do any harm,' said the Stanley trainer.

Akela turned to his Cubs. 'Cubs, how would you like to take on the famous Stanley Town Junior football team at cricket?'

'Cricket?' said Nobby.

'I'm game,' said Snowy.

'Yes, yes,' chanted the Cubs.

'Right, get the gear out of the mini-bus boot.'

Akela deliberately left his cricket gear in the boot of the mini-bus so that his Cubs could use it on any of their outings when the opportunity arose. So the cricket match was arranged, twenty-five overs each way. Billington Cubs were to bat first, and because Snowy was ready, Akela told him to open the batting. Chunky, the Stanley Town captain, paced out his bowling run.

Stanley Town were no fools at cricket. They played hard and fast. More than once Snowy was rapped hard on the pads by sharply turning balls bowled by Chunky. But gradually Billington, mainly by snatching singles, built up their score to twenty-nine.

Then Chunky bowled a full toss. This was too good an opportunity for Snowy to miss. He leapt down the pitch, swinging his bat, ready to lash the loose ball for six. For a moment he lost sight of the ball against the glare of the September sun. The ball whistled past his ear. Before Snowy could get back to his crease, the wicket-keeper had stumped him.

'Howzat!' screamed the wicket-keeper.

'Out!' said Akela, who was the bowling end umpire.

Billington were twenty-nine for nine wickets. Snowy walked off the field as Nobby waddled on.

'I'll knock 'im for six,' grinned Nobby as they passed.

'He bowls wicked off-breaks,' warned Snowy.

'Eh?' said Nobby.

'The ball breaks towards your leg!'

'Breaks your leg?' said Nobby.

Snowy walked on. It was not sporting to stay and discuss tactics with a player on his way to the wicket.

Snowy came in and took off his pads. He turned to watch Nobby at the wicket. Nobby had a most peculiar stance. He stood with his bat held right forward, towards the bowler, as if he was trying to shield his legs. It seemed he had taken Snowy's advice too seriously.

'Is that your stance?' said Akela.

Nobby nodded. Akela shrugged his shoulders.

'Play!' shouted Akela to the bowler.

Chunky ran up to bowl. The ball dropped on Nobby's off side, spun in and knocked down Nobby's wicket. Nobby did not move.

'Howzat!' screamed the wicket-keeper, twice in two balls.

'Out!' said Akela.

'Eh?' said Nobby, still holding his stance and squinting at the bowler.

'Out!' repeated Akela. 'You are out, bowled, middle stump.'

'I didn't see the ball.'

'That doesn't make any difference, you are still out.'

Nobby grunted. He walked off the field with the

other players. Billington were twenty-nine all out.
It was not a high score by any standard. Stanley
Town had done well to keep down the score. Now all
they had to do was to go all out for runs, and unless
they were very unlucky, they would get the thirty
runs they needed without any trouble.

'I didn't see the ball,' said Nobby to Snowy. 'All
I could see was the sun.'

Snowy nodded. He too had noticed the sun had
come up behind the bowler's hand. Perhaps he could
use it to his advantage.

Snowy placed his fielders around the bat, ready to
snap up any catch. He paced out his bowling run. He
noticed the batsman squinting at him in the strong
sunlight. Snowy also noticed his own long shadow.

The sun was now right behind him. He knew a high ball, with the sun behind it, would be virtually impossible to see.

That observation saved Billington. Snowy soon found a good length. When the batsman could play the ball, there was always a fielder ready to pounce in for a catch. When he could not play the ball, it usually knocked back a stump. The Stanley Town wickets fell. They were all out for 20. Billington had won.

'Yippee! Yippie! Yippie!' shrieked Nobby, as they drew out the stumps.

'Ah, you couldn't beat us at football,' said a Stanley player as they walked off the field.

'Oh, yes, we could,' said Nobby, before anyone could stop him.

'You want to prove it?'

'Anytime!' said Nobby. 'What about now?'

'My team are thirsty for revenge,' said Chunky to Snowy. 'We'd like to challenge you to a game of football sometime.'

'I don't mind,' said Snowy, not knowing how to refuse a challenge.

'Great! We'll leave it to the trainers to fix up a date, eh?'

'All right,' said Snowy reluctantly.

'It won't be for a while yet,' said Chunky. 'We've got a busy season ahead of us.'

'That's all right,' said Snowy. 'We don't mind waiting.'

As the Cubs parted, Akela caught Snowy by the shoulder.

'What . . . what were you talking about?' he choked.

'Stanley Town want to play us at football,' said Snowy.

'Football? Football?' shrieked Akela, almost in a panic.

'Yes,' said Snowy. 'Chunky said his team is thirsting for revenge.'

'Thirsting for revenge?' Akela sat on the mini-bus step and held his head in his hands.

'We couldn't refuse a challenge, could we?' said Snowy.

'Oh, oh!' groaned Akela. 'The 2nd Billington Cub Scout Pack will go down in the Book of Records – as the world's biggest losers!'

2 · The long trek

IN THE football match between the 2nd Billingtons and West Park, the 2nd Billingtons lost six–nil.

'We can't win them all,' said Akela, as his defeated team tramped off the field. 'Better luck next time. West Park were the better team. They ran like the wind, they jumped like gymnasts and they . . . they made that ball move like a cannon-ball.'

'We ran like old codgers, jumped like camels and made the ball move like a Christmas pudding,' groaned Nobby.

Akela laughed. 'You weren't that bad,' he said. 'You stood up to them, in fact I was rather proud of you. You never gave up from start to finish, and that is the spirit I like.'

'We can improve,' said Snowy. 'In a return match, I don't think West Park will have it so much their way.'

'Perhaps not,' said Akela. 'However, next week we are going on a sponsored walk.'

'Sponsored walk? What's a sponsored walk?' asked Nobby.

'In a sponsored walk, volunteers try to walk a certain distance – in our case, ten kilometres. They ask people, dads, mums, relations, friends, to sponsor them for the walk. Each sponsor agrees to pay the walker, say five pence for every kilometre he walks. So if the Cub walks ten kilometres, he will collect from that sponsor fifty pence, which he will pass on to the charity fund. It's a new craze around here. Everybody's doing it.'

'Which charity are we supporting?' asked Snowy.

'The Handicapped Children's Fund,' said Akela. 'It's to raise money for a swimming-pool for the handicapped kids.'

Snowy nodded. He knew the handicapped children would have the full support of the Billington Group.

At ten o'clock the next Saturday morning, the Cubs, along with Scouts, Guides, Brownies, parents and various officials were gathered outside their Headquarters. It was a bright, cool and gusty October morning. Giant white clouds were building up against the blue sky. If the weather should stay like this, it would be perfect for long distance walking.

Over a hundred boys and girls were ready to attempt their sponsored walks in aid of their favourite charity. Snowy had a dozen people sponsoring him for various amounts, which would bring him in £8.50, if he could complete his ten kilometre walk. Nobby would earn £4.50 and the other Cubs about £7 each on average.

Just then a noisy little racing-car in British racing green colours swerved through the entrance. As it screeched down the drive, it made groups of people jump out of the way. The young man in the driving seat wore a fixed grin like someone out of a toothpaste advertisement. All eyes were on him as he stepped out of his racing-car. He wore a yellow, hairy jacket, trousers made of printed cloth more suited to curtains and silver-sprayed button-up boots. He waved to the surrounding gatherings.

'It's Dicky Mickey,' crooned a Girl Guide to her companions.

The girls giggled.

'Hi, folks,' grinned Dicky Mickey.

Nobby nudged Snowy. 'Who ... who's Dicky Mickey?'

'Dicky Mickey?' said Snowy. He recognised the visitor from photographs he had seen in the newspapers. 'He's a radio disc jockey. He plays records on the early morning show sometimes. He cracks silly jokes like – question: What's up? Answer: An umbrella in the rain! Ugh! He's awful, but he does a lot of good work for charity.'

Several of the Scouts went up to welcome the visitor. Akela shook his hand.

'Hullo, Dick,' said Akela. 'Welcome back to Billington. I didn't know you were coming today.'

'When I heard you were doing this walk for charity, no one could keep me away,' said Dicky. 'I see you are still running your Cub Scout Pack, eh? Well, keep up the good work. You've got a good turn-out for the walk, I see. The handicapped kids' swimming-pool fund is a good cause, it really is. I wish you every success.'

'Are you joining us in the walk?'

Dicky Mickey laughed. 'I wish I could, I wish I could. How far do you intend to walk?'

'My Cubs will try to walk ten kilometres, same as the Guides,' said Akela. 'The Scouts are going for at least twenty-five kilometres, and I believe some of them are trying for up to fifty. Some of the Venture Scouts set off this morning, expecting to do a hundred!'

'That's great, that's really great,' said Dicky. 'I'd like to join you at the start, but I doubt if I could keep up with you.'

'You can walk with the Brownies,' said Nobby. 'They are only walking five kilometres.'

Dicky Mickey grinned. 'Good for them, good for them.'

A press photographer in the crowd took a series of photographs of the radio celebrity with the Cubs and Scouts, Brownies and Guides. Then the walkers, in their little groups of up to six, set off separately for their walks. Five parents had volunteered to walk with the Cubs, and they too set off on their ten kilometre treks.

The crowds gradually dispersed until only Dicky Mickey, a couple of press men and the Tawny Brown Six Cubs were left. Even Akela, who had agreed to walk with the Tawny Brown Six, was nowhere in sight. The photographer aimed his camera at Dicky posing with the Cubs looking at a map of their route.

Akela came back from the telephone box looking disappointed.

'Our walk will have to be delayed,' he said. 'One of the Venture Scouts has twisted his ankle near Wilmslow and I said I'd pick him up and take him home ...'

The Cubs groaned. They were all keyed up for their walk, and to have it delayed now did not suit them.

'Can I help?' said Dicky.

'You can't carry an injured passenger in your car, can you?'

'No, no,' said Dicky, 'it's only a single-seater, but I have a Rolls at home which can seat eight.'

'That's not much use to us now,' said Akela. 'I'll have to go off in the Scout mini-bus to pick up the injured Venture Scout. I won't be back for half-an-hour. If you will, I'd like you to go off with my Cubs. I'll catch up with you as soon as I can. Look, I've marked the route on the map. It's quite easy to follow and you'll have no problems with traffic. My Cubs are sensible in emergencies . . .'

'Yeah, all right,' said Dicky. 'I don't mind doing my bit.'

'If you have any trouble, just stay where you are until I catch up, all right?'

'Sure, sure. Don't worry about us. We'll make out fine.'

Akela then turned to his Cubs. 'Dicky Mickey is not only a radio star,' he said, 'but an ex-member of the 2nd Billington Scout Troop. He has kindly offered to stand in for me and start you on your walk until I catch up. I want you to give him your fullest co-operation, understand?'

The Cubs nodded. They were relieved their walk was not cancelled.

'Good!' Akela gave his map to Dicky Mickey and

had a few final words with him. Then Akela went off
to start the mini-bus.

'Well, what are we waiting for?' said Dicky. 'Let's
go! Tell me if I go too fast for you.'

Off he went through the gate with the Cubs following. He glanced at his map and turned off by the path
which followed the stream. They made slow progress.

'What goes ninety-nine-plonk?' said Dicky, moving along with a pronounced limp.

The Cubs did not answer. They wanted to save their
energies for their long walk ahead.

'A centipede with a wooden leg,' laughed Dicky.

He slapped his bright patterned trousers and
roared with laughter. The Cubs groaned.

Snowy doubted that at this rate they would ever
complete the course that day. The trouble was,
Dicky Mickey talked too much. Whenever he could,
he would stop and make a little joke, then he would
be off again. In this fashion, he told them all about
the walks he did in the Scouts with Akela, and all
about the records he played on his radio show.

By the time the party crossed West Park, Dicky
hobbled a little as if his shiny boots were too tight
for him. He sat down on a park bench. The Cubs
stood around waiting.

'My heel hurts,' said Dicky. He took off his boot
and sock. 'What have we here, why what do you
know, there's a nail sticking through the heel.'

He rubbed his sore foot. Snowy picked up the boot and felt inside. A nail was sticking out about two millimetres. It wasn't very sharp, but he could imagine it could be painful. He opened out the boot as far as he could and knocked it on the backpost of the park bench to knock down the nail. He felt inside the boot. It was now smooth.

'I've knocked the nail down,' said Snowy, handing back the boot to Dicky.

'Oh, thanks,' said Dicky. 'Those nails can be very painful, and you never know how dangerous they can be. I wouldn't want my heel to turn septic.'

'Is it all right now?' said Snowy, anxious to go on.

'It still hurts a bit. I think I'd better not risk going on. We'll wait for your Cub Scout Leader to catch up, then you can go on with him. Any other time, I'd be pleased to go along with you, but not today.'

The Cubs shrugged their shoulders and sat on the

grass to wait for Akela. Dicky looked up at the sky. Dark clouds were building up all around. He turned up his hairy coat collar.

'Looks like rain,' he said. 'Why do Spanish airmen always wear raincoats?'

No one answered.

'Because the rain in Spain falls mainly on their planes.'

No one laughed. Dicky stood up.

'We'd better get back before we are caught in a thunderstorm,' he said. 'Come on, Cubs, up you get. Follow me.'

'Go back?' said Snowy. 'But that means we won't collect the money for the handicapped children.'

'I know, I know, I know,' said Dicky. 'I don't like giving up either, but we can't go on if the weather turns bad.'

Dicky hobbled off. Snowy clenched his teeth. He would have walked on whatever the weather, but Dicky was their appointed leader. He was responsible for them, and Akela would be very annoyed with them if they did not co-operate. Snowy ambled after the others back to Group Headquarters.

It was still dry, but the thunderclouds continued to build up in the sky. The atmosphere felt humid and electric, as if there could be a downpour at any moment. However they reached Group Headquarters without being caught in the rain. Dicky trudged

into the hall, sat down, took off his boots and socks
and rubbed his feet.

'We probably got back just in time,' he said,
looking out of the window. 'In a few minutes, it will
be pelting down with rain.'

Just then Akela arrived back in the Scout mini-
bus. The Cubs went out to meet him.

'What . . . what are you lot doing here?' he gasped
in surprise. 'You should be half way round the course
by now.'

'Dicky Mickey said we should come back,' said
Snowy.

'Yeah, he had a sore heel and didn't want to get
wet,' said Nobby.

'We only crossed West Park,' said another Cub.

'We won't get any money for our walk.'

'Can we still go?'

Akela did not answer his Cubs. He went into the
hall just as the thunder crackled overhead.

'Have a spot of trouble, Dick?' asked Akela.

Dicky buttoned up his silver boots. 'Oh, nothing
much,' he said casually. 'I had a bit of a sore heel,
and the weather didn't look too good. It was better
in the circumstances to come back. You said I was
not to take any risks with your Cubs, and I didn't
want to get them wet through to the skin.'

'Quite right,' said Akela, looking out of the window
at the humid weather.

Again the thunder crackled overhead.

'There, what did I tell you,' chuckled Dicky. 'Before long it will be raining, pouring, chucking it down. You can't expect your Cubs to walk ten kilometres in this weather.'

'I don't expect my Cubs to do anything they don't want to do,' grunted Akela.

'But we want to finish this walk,' said Snowy. 'We want to raise money for the Handicapped Children's Fund.'

'In this weather?' Dicky laughed. 'You'd be far better off at home playing with your toy trains. No one will blame you for not going on this afternoon. In fact, I'm sure not one of you would really want to walk ten kilometres, not if it's raining.'

The Cubs remained silent. Not one of them agreed with the radio celebrity. Dicky turned to Akela. He laughed again.

'I bet you a pound per kilometre per Cub that they could not have completed the course this afternoon.'

Akela turned from the window. 'Are you sponsoring my Cubs for the walk?'

'Er, well, er, if you like, er, yes. I'm saying . . .'

Akela turned to his Cubs. 'This weather is not suitable for a walk . . .'

'We don't mind,' said Snowy. 'We want to raise some money for the handicapped children. A little rain won't do us any harm.'

'Who's for walking ten kilometres in this weather?' asked Akela.

The Cubs all put up their hands and crowded round Akela.

'Let's go, let's go,' they said.

'We're the only Six in the whole Group who aren't out walking,' said Snowy.

'Let's go, let's go, let's go!'

Akela frowned for a moment, then he looked up.

'The weather looks bad,' he said.

'We don't mind how bad it is,' said the Cubs.

'All right, we'll go!' Akela said simply.

The Cubs cheered.

'Form up outside,' said Akela. 'Here, Snowy, take the map. You lead the way. I'll come behind.'

Snowy led the way. The other Cubs were right behind him so he did not tarry. Off he went along the path they had travelled only half-an-hour before.

There was no sign that the threatening weather would hold off. Indeed, even before they had crossed West Park, they were caught in a downpour which drenched them all. Snowy walked on with head bent against the beating raindrops. It was useless attempting to talk. It was all he could do to keep on moving. He slithered and slipped on the muddy path. He had no idea how far ten kilometres was, certainly he had not walked that distance before. But the idea of turning back did not enter his head. He could see,

on the other side of the park, the pleasant buildings of the handicapped children's home. He was determined to earn every penny he could to support their fund.

The rain did not let up. When they reached the main road, they did not find any shelter, not that they looked for any. Snowy walked on with his head down. Even the trees overhanging the pavements dripped like showers. Rain beating off the stone flags splashed their legs. Pools formed in the road and gutters. Passing cars sprayed them with sheets of water.

On one occasion a large furniture van pulled up at the pavement beside them.

'Want a lift?' shouted the van driver through his cab window. 'There's plenty of room in the back.'

'What about it, Cubs?' shouted Akela.

'The 2nd Billingtons have their own transport,' shouted back Snowy, pointing to his legs.

The Cubs walked on. The van driver said something under his breath, withdrew into his cab and drove off. What was the use of a lift, thought Snowy. They were as wet as they could be. The rain could not harm them any more. All Snowy wanted to do was to walk ten thousand metres, and he would not be content to walk one step less. He would have to be chained down to stop him now. They walked on.

On another occasion, a police car stopped alongside.

'Are you lot mad?' shouted a policeman through the window.

'Sponsored walk for the Handicapped Children's Fund,' shouted back Akela.

'Oh!' said the policeman. 'Oh, best of luck!'

He closed his window and watched the rain-drenched party walk on.

The Cubs proceeded through the rain to over half-way round their route. Now their spirits were raised. It was a shorter distance to go on than to turn back.

Akela hurried up to the front of the line. He wiped the water off his face.

'We've got dry towels back at Group Head-quarters,' he said. 'You can have a warm shower if you wish and change into the Cub football shirts and shorts and socks. You can have a hot drink, and after that, I'll drive you home in the Scout mini-bus. You've earned it, every one of you.'

'I think we've earned our Swimmer Badges, too,'

said Nobby, making the arm movements of the breast stroke in the rain.

Another sheet of water was thrown at them by a passing car.

'We're Riding Along on the Crest of a Wave!' sang out Nobby.

They all joined in. The little party marched on, singing their hearts out. As the rain eased, they were able to lift up their heads and straighten their shoulders. They turned into the straight road which led to Group Headquarters. Their attempt would not be in vain.

They trudged on down the road, and it was only when their destination came in sight that they realised how tired they were. They squelched their way through the gates to the Cub hall. Dicky's little racing car was still parked in the drive, it's open cockpit now protected by a water-proof cover. However, Dicky himself was not around. The Cubs filed into the cloakroom to change out of their dripping wet clothes.

Akela made sure they were thoroughly dry and dressed in the warm football gear. He got them to brew up their hot chocolate drinks. He himself changed into one of his tracksuits he used for refereeing. They had no sausages, but they shared out their biscuits.

Akela totalled up the figures on the Cubs cards.

'Our little walk will bring in forty-two pounds, ten pence for the Handicapped Children's Fund,' he said.

'Why don't we go round twice and make it eighty-four pounds twenty pence?' chirped up Nobby.

Just then Dicky Mickey squelched in, wet through to the skin.

'Hi, folks,' he grinned.

'Where have you been?' said Akela, looking up. 'You're wet through. Come into the cloakroom and I'll find you a towel.'

'You've nearly drowned your hairy coat,' said Nobby.

'I nearly drowned myself,' said Dicky.

However, Dicky joined the Cubs around the stove for a hot drink. He soon, like the Cubs, recovered his strength.

'Did you complete your walk?' asked Dicky.

'Yes, every one of us,' said Akela, proudly, 'in spite of the rain.'

'And it was up-hill there and back,' said Nobby.

'Great, great, great! You certainly showed me what courage is,' said Dicky. 'When I saw you little 'uns go off in that terrible weather, I felt quite weak by comparison. I felt handicapped myself.'

'Have another hot chocolate to build up your strength. Pass the jug, Louie.'

Louie topped-up the visitor's mug with hot chocolate.

Dicky pulled out his cheque book and pen.

'Before I forget, let me settle my debts. Now what is six Cubs times ten kilometres times one pound?'

'Six hundred kilometres!' said Nobby.

'Sixty pounds,' corrected Snowy.

'Sorry, sixty pounds,' said Nobby. 'I'm not very good at sums.'

Dicky handed a cheque to Akela. Akela read it and frowned.

'Seventy pounds?' he said.

'That's right,' said Dicky. 'When I saw your Cubs put themselves out for the handicapped kids, I just had to do it myself. I sponsored myself, and what do you know? I completed the course!'

'The complete course?' asked Akela.

'Every step of it,' grinned Dicky.

After that, the Cubs did not think Dicky Mickey was such a bad sport.

3 · Furious flood

THE early November fields were wet and muddy. The Cubs were so black after their Saturday morning football practice match that it was difficult to tell the difference between the white and red shirts.

'You played well in spite of the heavy ground,' said Akela, as they ambled back to Group Headquarters, 'but remember, you can't kick a heavy ball far, and you must play closer together in these conditions. As for you, Nobby, when you've got nothing to do in the goalmouth, don't roll in the puddles.'

Akela ushered his Cubs through the rear entrance of Group Headquarters.

'Our next football practice will be next Saturday morning as usual, but this afternoon, I have another sport for some of you to try.'

'Oh, what's that? What's that?' said the Cubs, crowding round Akela.

'I'll tell you after you've had a shower,' grinned Akela, keeping his Cubs in suspense.

Indeed, Akela waited until his Cubs had all showered, changed and each one had a mug of hot cocoa before he broke the news.

'The Scouts are taking out their new rowing-boat this afternoon,' said Akela. 'It's very fast. It's an eight-oar rowing-boat. I doubt if there's a faster one of its size in Cheshire.'

The Cubs pricked their ears. Whatever the Scouts did usually affected the Cubs later. Snowy had seen the long, slim rowing-boat gradually take shape, as the Scouts built it. So far, however, none of the Cubs had joined in any boating activities.

'The Scouts are planning to race next season,' said Akela. 'They say they need some practice at over-taking another rowing-boat, so I volunteered . . .'

The Cubs cheered. They knew what was coming next. They knew Akela would miss no opportunity to get his Cubs in on the big boy acts.

'. . . I volunteered the services of the 2nd Billington Cub Scouts.'

The Cubs clapped their hands. Akela waited for silence before he proceeded.

'This afternoon, I want six Cubs to crew the spare six-oar rowing-boat . . . Put your hands down, I'll choose the crew when I'm ready. I want six Cubs to crew the spare rowing-boat on Earlestown Canal. I shall be cox, that is the man at the back of the boat who calls out the time and does the steering.

The Scouts will give us a start, then they'll practise overtaking us in the narrow canal.' Akela's eyes twinkled. 'But I intend the Cubs to keep ahead and reach the winning line before the Scouts.'

The Cubs cheered again.

'As for the crew . . .'

Little Nobby put up his hand. 'May I be one of the crew, please?'

'No, not this time,' said Akela, sharply. 'I want only the best swimmers first.'

'I . . . I can nearly swim,' said Nobby.

Akela ignored him. 'I want the six best swimmers. I have chosen the team from those who have their Swimmer Badges. These are:' (Akela read from a list) 'Snowy White, Bobbie Smith, Fletch, Tony, Mick Munroe, and Louie Watson.'

Nobby put up his hand. 'May I be a passenger?'

'No,' said Akela.

'Would you . . . would you mind if I was a stow-away?' whispered Nobby.

'I don't want to see you touch a boat this afternoon,' said Akela, 'or any other day for that matter. Not until you have your Swimmer Badge.'

'May I watch?' said Nobby, desperately. 'May I have just a little peep?'

Akela frowned. 'Well, I can't stop anyone just watching, but I will not take any non-swimmers on the water, and that's final.'

Snowy put up his hand. 'I shan't be coming this afternoon,' he said. 'I promised to stay and help Nobby mend a puncture.'

'He's always getting punctures. He never stops getting punctures. Help him mend his punctures this morning. You've had your Swimmer Badge nearly two years now, Snowy. I need you in the Cub crew. I mean to give the Scouts a good run, and I hope you won't let the Pack down.'

Snowy did not like leaving his friend, Nobby, but on the other hand, he did not want to let his Pack down.

'Don't mind me, Snowy,' said Nobby, unselfishly. 'You go. Maybe I'll be in the crew next year. I'll come along and watch.'

'All right, I'll come,' said Snowy.

Akela then went on to give precise instructions to the crew he had chosen for that afternoon's practice. The Cubs listened. They knew Akela was fair and would give them all the chance to go rowing as soon as he could, as soon as they had their Swimmer Badges.

That afternoon, the Cub and Scout rowing crews piled into their assorted vehicles. Nobby snuggled into the back corner seat of the mini-bus, hoping no one would notice him. Akela counted the heads of his crew and found them all correct. Outside, the Scout Leader checked that the two rowing-boats (the eight-oar boat and the spare six-oar boat) were securely mounted on their trailer, then he waved away the towing vehicle, a borrowed Land Rover. The Scout Leader climbed into his own little car with some of his Scouts, and drove off after the boats. Akela started the mini-bus engine and drove off after the others.

The canal had much improved after the building of Denby Sluice earlier that year. The new sluice looked rather like a combined concrete dam and weir and was used for regulating the waters of the canal. In the concrete structure were openings in which were mounted the sluice gates themselves. The sluice gates were metal doors which were opened to let the canal waters through when the canal waters were too high, or closed to help maintain the height of the canal waters behind. The whole structure was topped by a metal cat-walk, from where spectators could watch the calm canal waters on one side, slowly drift into a waterfall tumbling over the top of the concrete weir, or gush through the open sluice gates below, in a glittering crescendo of moving water.

In the mini-bus, Cubs and Scouts sang their Troop song, 'Riding Along on the Crest of a Wave', with gusto, for it seemed appropriate that day in particular. The strong voices of the Scouts seemed to fill the whole mini-bus. Anyway, it made the journey pass very quickly, for they only stopped singing when they came within sight of the canal.

'Isn't it quiet without that little Nobby?' said Akela.

'Pardon?' said Nobby from the back of the mini-bus.

Akela turned and goggled at his little Cub.

'I . . . I didn't see you board the bus,' he said. 'What . . . what are you doing here?'

'I . . . I came to watch. I came to cheer you on. You . . . you said I could watch.'

Akela was at a loss for words. He slumped limply into his seat.

All the vehicles came to a halt on the gravel beside the canal slipway. Already the Scouts who had travelled with the Scout Leader had unlashed the boats from the trailer. The weather was rough and windy.

After the recent heavy thunderstorms, the canal was full, almost overflowing its banks. It seemed that the new sluice couldn't get the floods away fast enough. But it was sunny, and the crews got ready for their sport. They hauled out their kit, life-jackets, oars and baling-out sponges. Akela caught Nobby by the tail of his jersey.

'I know you are very keen to join in all Cub activities,' he said, 'but I don't want you to go within three paces of the canal edge, understand? You know canals can be dangerous, don't you?'

'Yes,' said Nobby, meekly.

'Take the spare life-jacket,' said Akela. 'You can sit in the mini-bus if you want to. There's a pile of *Scout* magazines and books you can borrow. I'll get them for you. You can read, can't you?'

'Oh, thanks,' said Nobby. 'I can read comics.'

Akela got the magazines for Nobby. He sat him in the mini-bus and closed the door. Outside, Akela heaved a sigh of relief.

'That little menace gives me nightmares,' he said to the Scout Leader. 'It wouldn't surprise me if he ran the mini-bus into the canal. I'll chock the wheels to be safe, and hide the ignition keys.'

By this time, the Scouts had launched the boats. Akela got his crew in their positions in the six-oar rowing-boat, and again explained to them the rudiments of rowing. Then all was ready. The Cub boat was pushed away from the bank, and drifted in the deep waters of the canal. The Cubs were afloat for the first time. They practised their first strokes, and under the guidance of Akela, they soon got the hang of it. The boat slid through the water like a sleek glider through air.

The Scouts were ready to practise their overtaking manoeuvre, so they let the Cubs get away first.

'Heave! Heave! Heave!' called Akela, as they slid under a low iron footbridge which spanned the canal. 'Don't dip your oar too deeply, Bobbie. Take your oar farther back, Mick. Match your stroke to Snowy's. Heave! Heave! Heave!'

The Cub boat sped away past the Sea Cadet H.Q. on the left bank, and away along a long straight. Snowy bent his back to his oar. It was a great feeling to pull on an oar with all his might, and the boat moved so smoothly, so swiftly and so quietly. This was moving! It seemed as if they stood a good chance of staying ahead of the Scouts after all.

'Away, Cubs, away,' yelled a squeaky voice from the canal bank.

Snowy looked up and saw Nobby waving him on from the tow-path. Akela groaned.

'What's he up to now?'

'Away, the 2nd Billington Cubs! The Scouts are nowhere in sight. Yes, they are. They're just coming round the bend. Away, Cubs away!'

The Cubs strained on their oars. Snowy looked up and saw the Scouts about thirty metres behind. Akela glanced back over his shoulder to keep an eye on them too – not that that was necessary, for Nobby, on the tow-path, kept them all fully informed.

'They're catching up,' yelled Nobby. 'Away, the Cubs!'

However, the Cubs rowed very well, for Nobby, on the tow-path, had to run to keep up with them. Nevertheless, the Scouts steadily gained on them.

'Hurry up, hurry up, hurry up!' screeched Nobby from the tow-path, as if his life depended on the result of that race.

Akela steered his boat well, and he cut off corners at the bends whenever he could. But there was another straight stretch ahead, leading down to Denby Sluice. This straight was where the Scouts intended to pass the Cubs. However, the last bend before the straight was flooded. Akela headed for the shallows, hoping to gain a few more metres by a short cut, and still make a race of it.

The Cubs' boat slid over the shallows, with the Scouts' boat now only two lengths behind. Two oars struck the bottom.

'Not so deeply,' warned Akela. 'Just get your blades under the water. That's right. That's right. Heave! Heave! Heave!'

The Cubs heaved for all they were worth, and

their boat slid out of the shallows into the deeper stretch of water. Snowy noticed the Scouts were following them through the shallows, instead of going round the wide bend of the canal where the water was deeper.

'The Scouts are stuck,' yelled Nobby from the bank.

True enough, the heavier Scout crew was grounded in the shallows. They were stuck, hard and fast.

Akela glanced over his shoulder. The Scouts were in no danger, but now the Cubs, afloat in deep water, had a real advantage. They had only a hundred metres to go to the finishing line. There was a possibility

that they could reach it before the Scouts got themselves afloat again and caught up.

'Heave! Heave! Heave! Heave! Heave!' yelled Akela, at the top of his voice, as if everyone in the world was deaf to his words.

'Away, Cubs!' shrieked Nobby from the tow-path. 'Cubs away, away, away!'

The Cubs put every ounce of effort into their stroke. They slid down the centre of the canal. With every stroke, their confidence grew. With every stroke, the chances of winning grew. The Scouts were still grounded! It was impossible now for the Cubs to lose. They put more effort into their strokes to make

sure of their victory. The six-oar boat slid over the
finishing line first.

'We've won, we've won, we've won!' yelled Nobby,
dancing on the bank like a chimpanzee.

The Cubs slumped over their oars, thoroughly
exhausted by their efforts. But Akela did not seem
to be at all interested in their victory. He looked
towards Denby Sluice, near which drifted an un-
manned coal-barge.

'What's . . . what's going on there?' he mumbled
to himself. He shouted out an order. 'Pick up your
oars, Cubs. Heave, heave, heave!'

The Cubs rowed as best they could, and Akela
steered the boat for the bank. Snowy could now see
what the trouble was. A coal-barge had broken away
from its moorings upstream and had been carried by
the wind straight at the sluice wall. Snowy held his
breath as he watched the coal-barge bump into the
top of the sluice and buckle the metal cat-walk above.

Akela ran the rowing-boat on to the gently sloping
bank and leapt out.

'Pull the boat ashore,' he yelled to his Cubs.

He stayed only long enough to make sure that his
Cubs were all safely ashore, then he dashed off to the
sluice, to prevent any further damage, if he could.

Snowy saw Akela run along the buckled cat-walk
on top of the sluice until he was level with the cockpit
of the drifting coal-barge. The huge rudder flapped

about like a whale's tail. Each time it moved, the stern of the coal-barge swung first one way, then the other. The coal-barge was pounding the sluice like a giant sledge-hammer. If nothing was done, both the sluice and the coal-barge would be further damaged.

Akela leapt on to the coal-barge. His intention was quite clear to Snowy. If he could stop the coal-barge rudder flapping, he would bring the barge under control.

Akela held on to the swaying deck like a cat, but the coal-barge tiller, the handle connected to the rudder, swung across and cracked him across the knees. Akela was thrown off-balance, and when the barge swung out again, he fell into the canal. It looked as if he would be crushed between the coal-barge and the sluice.

'Call the Scouts to help Akela,' shouted Snowy to his fellow Cubs, as he darted away to the sluice, to help if he could.

Nobby, too, had seen the danger, and was already on the cat-walk.

'Swim, swim, swim,' Nobby yelled down to Akela. He made swimming motions in the air with his hands.

The coal-barge swung in on Akela. Nobby covered his face with his hands. Where Akela was at this time, Snowy could not see, but he was somewhere between the coal-barge rudder and the sluice. Nobby looked down again, closed his eyes, nipped his nose, pulled an imaginary chain and leapt into the canal.

When Snowy got on the sluice cat-walk, the coal-barge again crashed in, sending a shudder through the metal structure. For one moment, Snowy thought the whole cat-walk would be swept away over the weir. But what worried Snowy most of all was the appearance, in the concrete structure below, of a black, jagged crack, about a centimetre wide. Immediately, Snowy remembered the warnings the police had issued to motorists, about sudden damage caused by mining subsidence. If mining subsidence could crack roads, it could also crack dams, lock-gates, or, on this occasion, the new Denby Sluice.

In the water, Snowy saw Akela by the flapping rudder. Behind him, bobbing like a cork in his bright yellow life-jacket, was Nobby, trying to pull Akela clear. Snowy thought that if he could board the barge, and swing the rudder away, the two in the water could get out. Out of the corner of his eyes, he saw,

down the canal tow-path, the Scouts running up to help, but Snowy had to do what he could there and then.

The crack in the concrete structure widened. The metal cat-walk shuddered as the coal-barge crashed into it and knocked Snowy clean off his feet. Almost in slow motion, the concrete structure below broke apart, as Snowy tumbled into the open cockpit of the coal-barge.

There was a crash like a house collapsing as the middle of the sluice fell away. Tons of water wrenched their way through the breach. Snowy grabbed the tiller just as the heavy barge slid backwards, like a tank down a waterfall.

The coal-barge shot down foaming rapids, swirling like a cork. For a while it refused to answer to the tiller. Snowy swung the tiller hard to one side, and eventually the barge veered round to point downstream. In all this fury, Snowy could see no sign of Akela and Nobby.

Downstream, on the starboard side, was a shallow bank of shrubs. It looked the safest place to run aground, if Snowy could make it. He hauled over his tiller. The barge answered and yawed to the right in the raging stream. It skidded into the bank, the bow struck first and the barge swung into a giddy ground loop and scythed up the shallow bank. The barge flattened the bank of shrubs and crunched to a halt, flinging Snowy off his feet against the cockpit wall.

The raging flood outside roared, but now Snowy was conscious of the barge being absolutely still. The barge was grounded. Snowy stood up on the gunwales and looked around. He saw the pent up waters of the canal pour in a torrent through the broken sluice. The column of glassy water spread out into foaming rapids to overflow the banks and carry all before it. An up-rooted pine tree swirled in the waters.

Suddenly Snowy saw Akela and Nobby lying on the bank about fifty metres downstream. Snowy jumped ashore. He leapt fences and walls and charged through bushes and hedges to reach them. He found Nobby lying face down. Akela knelt beside him and applied artificial respiration. He was pumping spurts of water out of Nobby's mouth.

'Can I help?'

'Artificial respiration,' croaked Akela, in a voice hardly stronger than a whisper.

Snowy took over where Akela had left off. He knew the drill well enough. Akela had shown him plenty of times during first aid demonstrations. This left Akela free to sort himself out. Akela put his head between his knees and coughed up some of the canal water he had swallowed.

Nobby groaned. He would recover. Snowy continued his artificial respiration drill until Nobby pushed him away.

'Oh!' groaned Nobby. 'Leave me alone.'

'You'll be all right now,' said Snowy.

By this time, the emergency services, police, fire-brigade and ambulances had been alerted. Even the Sea Cadet Corps had turned out of their headquarters up by the iron bridge to give assistance. Three cadets appeared first on the scene.

'Need any help?' asked the Sea Cadet Commander. 'You're wet through. Come with us to our head-quarters and dry out.'

'Thanks,' said Akela. 'Lead the way.'

Akela and Nobby squelched away, in the company of Snowy and the Sea Cadets. By this time, the torrent through the broken sluice had almost stopped. What was left of the sluice effectively coped with what was left of the canal waters behind. As for the canal, its waters had dropped almost two metres. This was very noticeable where the Scout rowing-boat had run aground. What had been a wide expanse of shallow water a little while earlier, was now completely high and dry. The Scout boat was grounded on dry land.

The Sea Cadet headquarters was only a few metres downstream of the iron footbridge. Already the Cadets were preparing for their visitors. The wash-room was put at their disposal and dry towels, blankets and warm clothes laid out for them. A pot-bellied cast-iron stove glowed with heat.

By the time Akela and Nobby were back to normal, news came through that the crisis was almost over. Other weirs and lock-gates in the canal system had minimised the flood effects. Outside the Sea Cadet base, the canal was low, but quite calm. But the water was still deep enough to float a boat; in fact, the four Sea Cadet boats were milling about in the now quiet waters. The two Scout rowing-boats were lying on the slipway, where the Scout Leader had got his Cubs and Scouts to berth them.

'How would you like to row back to the mini-bus?' said the Scout Leader, as Akela came on to the quayside.

'Good idea,' said Akela. 'We have to go back to the mini-bus, so why not row? Cubs, launch your boat and take your places.'

The two rowing-boats were launched and the crews took their places. Nobby put his hands in his pockets and walked away.

'Hey, where are you going?' Akela shouted after him.

Nobby turned. 'To . . . to the mini-bus,' he said.

'So are we. Climb aboard!'

Akela pointed to a space in the rowing-boat just in front of him. Nobby stood at the top of the slip-way.

'But . . . but . . . but I haven't got my Swimmer Badge,' he said. 'I . . . I can't swim!'

'You've got a life-jacket, and you can swim well enough to jump into the canal to save me,' said Akela. 'Climb aboard. The convoy is awaiting your commands, admiral.'

Nobby climbed into the seat of honour. Akela handed him the cords which controlled the rudder. The boats pushed off and formed a line.

'Tell them when you're ready to go,' whispered Akela in Nobby's ear. 'Tell them when to go.'

'Ready, steady, go!' shouted Nobby.

'Ready, steady, go?' echoed Akela.

'I mean paddle,' said Nobby.

'Oar,' corrected Akela.

'Or what?' said Nobby, looking back at Akela.

'Give them the time,' said Akela.

Nobby turned around. 'I haven't got a watch, but it must be about half-past three.'

'No, no, no. Tell them to heave, heave, heave in time.'

'Heave, heave, heave,' yelled Nobby. 'Hurry up, you galley slaves or I'll have you all hung from the yardarm.'

In spite of this confusion, the convoy settled down to a steady pace. First came the Cub six-oar boat, captained by Nobby, then the Scout eight-oar, then the Sea Cadets' four boats in a line. It was the Cubs' day, but it was Nobby's hour. He was in command of the whole convoy.

'Heave, heave, heave,' yelled Nobby, as they approached the iron footbridge before them.

Nobby looked up at the spectators on the footbridge and waved.

'Where has all the canal water gone?' an old lady spectator asked her companion, looking down at the unusually low water level.

Nobby burped. 'I drank it,' he said.

4 · The frozen north

FOOTBALL, swimming, boating, running and walking were so far the main Cub sports that winter. As for the yoga exercises, they were not so welcome, and yet, of all sports, a half-hour introduction to the mysteries of this Eastern custom was worth more to Snowy than all the time he had ever spent chasing an English ball.

It was way back in September when Akela introduced his Pack to yoga. His Cubs were on their best behaviour that evening, for they had a lady visitor.

'This evening,' said Akela hoarsely, as he shuffled uneasily in his big shoes, 'we have Lady Mary Anne of Hazel Grove, who has kindly come along to give us a yoga demonstration.'

'Yoga?' said Nobby. 'That's like rice-pudding, isn't it?'

'That's sago,' said Snowy.

'Oh!' said Nobby. 'I like sago. How can anyone have a sago demonstration?'

'Yoga, I said,' said Akela, gruffly.

Lady Mary Anne smiled sweetly. She wore a smart blue cape. She stood as attractive as a ballerina, waiting patiently beside Akela for her turn to speak.

'I don't know anything about yoga, myself,' went on Akela, 'so I will enjoy this demonstration as much as you will, so give Lady Mary Anne your attention for the next half-hour. Lady Mary Anne . . .'

Akela stepped back to leave the floor to Lady Mary Anne.

'Would you like to join us?' said Lady Mary Anne, waving her hand to a vacant position on the floor.

'No, no, no, no, no,' said Akela, in embarrassment. 'I've . . . I've . . . I've got my register to mark and other things. I'll just stay in the background to make sure my Cubs behave themselves, eh? Ha, ha!'

He slunk off to a corner before Lady Mary Anne could reply. She shrugged her shoulders, took off her cape, draped it over a chair, and turned to face her class. Now she was dressed in a black leotard, that is a tight one-piece garment like a bathing-suit, in which ballerinas do their training.

'Yoga,' she said, in a clear voice, 'is a way to provide a healthy body and a healthy mind.' She spoke the Queen's English like the Queen herself. 'My husband and I learnt a little of this mysterious art when we stayed in India as guests of the Maharishi of Rangipore.'

With that, Lady Mary Anne bent down from the waist, and put the palms of her hands flat on the floor. She looked up at the Cubs, raised her feet off the ground, and bent her body so her feet were resting on top of her head. The Cubs gasped. They could hardly believe their eyes.

'One branch of yoga is concerned with a number of physical exercises called asanas. The asana I'm doing now is called the Scorpion.'

Lady Mary Anne uncoiled herself, put her feet gently on the ground and stood upright. She sat on the floor, and put her feet behind her ears. She pressed down her hands to raise herself clear of the floor.

'This asana is called the Spider Crab,' she said, and holding this peculiar position, she walked round the room on her hands. 'These stretching exercises tone up certain muscles in the body far more effectively than any other sport such as tennis or hockey.'

Lady Mary Anne returned to the head of the room and uncoiled herself. She stood on her head, and placed her hands by her sides so she was supported on nothing more than the crown of her head.

'Other exercises such as this,' she went on, 'improve the blood circulation, and a good blood circulation benefits every part of the body, the muscles, internal organs and the brain.'

Lady Mary Anne swung her legs around like the

sails of a windmill, so she spun like a top on the crown of her head before lowering herself into a sitting position. She crossed her legs.

'Other exercises improve the breathing system.'

She breathed first through one nostril, then the other.

'She sounds like an old drainpipe,' Nobby whispered to Snowy.

'So you see, yoga exercises improve the state of the muscles, the blood circulation, the breathing system and all parts of the body. It results in a healthy body and a healthy mind.'

Every Cub in the hall, and Akela himself, watched this yoga demonstration completely fascinated.

'Now we'll try a few simple exercises together, shall we?' said Lady Mary Anne.

As soon as she said that, Akela coughed, took a pile of papers from the table drawer and pretended to read them.

'Let us start with the exercise called "Salute to the Sun",' she said. 'Now, everybody, stretch up like this.'

The Cubs stretched up their hands to the ceiling like Lady Mary Anne.

'Stretch up and bow down to Salute the Sun.'

Nobby looked over his shoulder.

'How can we Salute the Sun when we can't even see it? I can't even see the sky! Anyway, it's dark outside, and it's been raining all day. I haven't seen the sun for a fortnight.'

'Don't ask such silly questions,' grunted Akela from his corner.

'Pretend you are standing in a glorious blaze of sunlight, dear boy,' said Lady Mary Anne.

'Glorious blaze of rhubarb,' muttered Nobby, as he bent down. His little bones creaked like rusty door hinges.

Snowy pressed his hands down on the floor, and felt all his back muscles, from heels to shoulders, being gently stretched. His face was flushed with the effort. He slipped down his woggle to loosen his scarf to give himself more room to manoeuvre and to breathe.

'Now stand on one leg like a Stork,' said Lady Mary Anne, 'and bend down slowly . . .'

Lady Mary Anne led the Cubs through a whole series of exercises, the Locust, the Archer, the Bow, the Crab and others too numerous to mention here. The Cubs tied themselves in all kinds of knots. On one occasion, Nobby got his left foot stuck behind his neck and had to be untied by Akela.

'What was that exercise called?' said Nobby, as he was disentangled. 'A Greek Vase? It should have been called a Round Turn and Two Half Hitches, if you ask me!'

Finally the Cubs ended up doing headstands and

were shown how to roll out of these positions without hurting themselves. In fact, they enjoyed headstands so much that they did them in their own time. They flicked up and down all over the floor, like magic beans, until Akela came among them to sort them out.

'Stop messing about!' he growled. 'Get back to your places.'

The Cubs calmed down. After these yoga exercises, Snowy felt as if his body had been stretched on the rack in all directions, but he suffered not the slightest ill-effect.

'Well, that is an introduction to yoga,' concluded Lady Mary Anne. 'I'm sure you will now agree that these exercises really do tone up the muscles, improve the blood circulation and breathing system and help to give you a healthy body and a healthy mind.'

Akela thanked Lady Mary Anne on behalf of his Cubs. He helped her on with her cape, escorted her to her little car outside and with his Cubs, waved goodbye.

'Well, that's yoga,' said Akela as he returned to the hall. 'What do you think of it?'

The Cubs shrugged their shoulders. They did not know what to think about yoga.

'I've heard some strange tales about yoga,' went on Akela. 'I've heard that yogis can sit in the snow, and by doing yoga exercises, can melt the snow in a circle around them. I don't know how true that is . . . there are many strange tales in the world . . .' Akela looked at his watch. 'Anyway, to return to more familiar subjects, Cub games, we just have time for a quick game of volley-ball before flag down. Cubs, form Sixes!'

The Cubs formed their Sixes and were organised into teams to play volley-ball. That might have been the end of their yoga activity, had it not been for a tragic event which occured one icy December evening, nearly four months later. Strangely enough, on that eventful evening, the Cubs had played another game of volley-ball before flag down. Snowy and Nobby walked home together after their Friday Cub night. It was dark, cold, and the ground was icy.

'What are you doing tomorrow, Snowy, playing football?' asked Nobby.

'Sure, after I've been to the library. Are you coming?'

'You bet!'

'Pity the evenings are so dark, or we'd be able to play more football. I'd like to have another match with West Park, to make up for our six–nil defeat . . . Hey, Nobby, what's this?'

At that time, the Cubs were passing by a large cattle truck parked under a street lamp. From the truck came a pathetic bleat of a sheep or goat. One of the frost-covered side planks of the truck was broken, and through it protruded a little hoofed foot. The foot was wedged in the broken side plank and it was apparent that the animal was in pain. Snowy looked in the cab but saw no sign of the driver.

'Poor thing,' said Nobby. 'What . . . what can we do?'

'Help it quickly,' said Snowy.

Snowy ran round to the back of the truck, unfastened the catches and let the tailboard drop. In the glimmer of the light from the street lamp, he saw a kid goat wedged in the corner of the truck.

Snowy leapt up on the tailboard to go to its aid. What he saw almost made him feel sick.

The kid goat was tied by a rope around its neck. It had been alone in the truck, apart from a few farming tools, including a lawn mower. During the journey, the lawn mower had rolled on to the animal, which, in trying to get free, had almost strangled itself. In desperation, the animal had kicked out with its hind feet, to break one of the planks in which it had caught its leg.

'Give me a hand to move this mower,' said Snowy to Nobby.

They lifted the mower off the animal, then Snowy

prised back the broken plank to free the injured leg.
Nobby loosened the rope round the kid goat's neck.
He picked up an overturned tin bowl.

'Its drinking water is frozen,' he said. 'How . . .
how can anyone be so cruel?'

Snowy made the goat as comfortable as he could.
The kid's leg was cut and still bleeding although the
congealed blood showed that the animal had been in
pain for many hours. Snowy unzipped his fur-lined
anorak, pulled up his Cub jersey and pulled out his
shirt tail. He tore a strip off the bottom of his shirt
tail, and used it as a bandage for the injured leg.
Finally he wrapped it up in his Cub scarf.

'This animal needs a vet,' said Snowy, 'and quickly.'

Just then Snowy heard footsteps on the pavement.
Before he could leap out, he heard the engine start
and the gear lever pushed into position. Fearing he
would be left behind, if he jumped out, he stayed in
the back of the truck as the vehicle pulled away.

'We'll have to wait until he stops again.' said Snowy.

But apart from a momentary stop at an amber
traffic light, the indications were that the truck was
not going to stop. It turned on to the M6 motorway
at junction eighteen, and headed north, at a hundred
kilometres per hour, for Scotland.

'Where are we going, where are we going?' yelled
Nobby, against the roar of the engine.

'I don't know!' shouted back Snowy.

The bitter wind cut through the slats in the side of the truck and almost froze them to the bone. The kid goat shivered on the floor. Snowy now took off his fur-lined anorak and wrapped it round the kid goat. Nobby did the same, although that left him exposed to the bitter wind too. Their thin Cub jerseys did nothing to keep out the biting cold wind.

'My Dad said if I wasn't home by half-past nine, he'd leave me in the dog kennel for the night,' said Nobby. 'What can we do?'

'We can't wave to the cars behind from the back of the truck,' said Snowy. 'At this speed, and with the tailboard down, we might fall out. Besides, if we did get a message to a motorist behind, it would do no good. Vehicles mustn't stop on the motorway. If he tried to wave down our truck driver, he might cause a pile up. It's too dangerous. We'll have to sit it out until the truck stops.'

'We'll freeze to death,' said Nobby, snuggling down in a corner.

'Y . . . y . . . you might be right,' shivered Snowy.

It was difficult for him to speak, for his teeth chattered almost out of control. His shivers made his whole body tremble. Across his back, where he sat in the draught, was a pain as if a heavy sword was cutting into him.

'W . . . w . . . we've g . . . got t . . . to do s . . . something,' he shivered.

'W . . . w . . . w . . . what . . .?' said Nobby.

Snowy did not know. His brain, like the rest of his body, was becoming numb. It was difficult for him to think, and yet, in the depths of his mind, there stirred a memory. He remembered the story Akela told him, way back last September, about yogis being able to melt snow with their bodies.

'Y . . . y . . . yoga,' said Snowy. 'We'll . . . d . . . do y . . . yoga!'

'Y . . . yoga? Oh, y . . . yoga!'

'W . . . what L . . . lady what's-her-name showed . . . us!'

Snowy stretched his legs straight out on the truck floor, and bent his body so that his head touched his knees, in the pose of a Shrimp. He rolled over so he was face up, pressed his arms down to arch his back and threw back his head in the pose of a Locust. Next he bent back his legs and caught hold of his ankles, to bend himself like a Bow. He panted from his exertions.

'Try these yoga exercises, Nobby,' he said. 'It's our only chance to stop us freezing solid.'

Nobby groaned as he went through the motions. Every movement they made was agony. Their efforts made them quite exhausted, but Snowy encouraged them on.

They did all the yoga asanas they could remember, as best they could, and when they could remember no

more, they tried all the exercises again – backwards.
They did not melt any ice, but they kept going until
the truck turned off into a service station. Snowy
jumped up as the truck slowed down.

'We're stopping, we're stopping!' he yelled in
relief, and to his even greater relief, he saw a police
car conveniently positioned to observe the vehicles
coming into the service station.

The truck stopped in the car park. The driver
jumped out and went off to the café, but Snowy was
not interested in him for the moment.

'Watch the kid goat, till I get back with the police.'

Snowy ran to the police car, taking care to avoid
any vehicles which might be coming in.

'Och, wha' are ye doin' oot the nicht, laddie?' said
a burly policeman in a strong Scottish accent.

'There's an animal in trouble there,' said Snowy,
pointing back to the truck. 'Can you come, please?'

Snowy explained to the policemen, as they walked
back to the truck, how he and Nobby had seen the
goat's leg sticking out of the broken plank of the
truck, how they had climbed into the truck to free it,
and how the truck had driven off with them before
they could warn the truck driver. The policemen
listened calmly until they saw the pitiful animal,
then they were visibly shaken. The policeman's lip
quivered as he unclipped his pocket radio.

'Q-seven to control,' he said. 'Send a vet tae Glen

Cleekie service station, an' tell 'im tae bring his gun, or whatever he uses tae put animals oot of their misery.'

'You're . . . you're not going to . . .' said Snowy.

'That's no' for me to say, laddie,' said the policeman.

Snowy lowered his head. If the vet did put the little goat to sleep, all their efforts to save it would have been in vain. But Nobby apparently had not heard the policeman's last remark. He looked about him.

'Is this Scotland?' he said.

'Aye, this is Scotland,' said the other policeman.

'I've never been to Scotland,' said Nobby. 'What's it like?'

'Were're ye from, laddie?'

'England,' said Nobby.

'Cheshire,' said Snowy, more precisely. He shivered in the cold night air.

'Wah, that's over two hundred kilometres awa'. Ye're shivering, laddie. Come into the car and warm up.'

The policeman put the Cubs in the back of the police car and gave them blankets to wrap round them. Only when Snowy felt the warm air from the heater circulate round him did he realise how cold he had been. Nobby rubbed the steamed up windows and peered out. They saw another police car drive in escorting another car, presumably the vet's.

'How will we get back home?' said Nobby.

Snowy shrugged his shoulders. 'I don't know, Nobby.'

Just as Snowy was finally thawing out, the policemen returned to the car.

'I've got gud news for ye, laddies,' he said, handing back their anoraks. 'The vet says that the goat is such a fine animal that he'll dae wha' he can tae save her.' The policemen climbed into their seats. 'Noo we'll see about gettin' ye hame tae your folks.'

'My Dad said he'd lock me in the dog kennel tonight if I'm not in by half-past nine.'

The policeman looked at his watch and laughed.

'It's half-past midnight, noo,' he said, 'but dinna

worry aboot your father. Ye'll be 'is pride and joy
when we tell 'im wha' heroes ye've been tae-nicht.'

The police car glided out of the service station just
as Snowy saw the truck driver being bundled into
the other police car. They sped down the motorway.
Their journey south was much more comfortable than
their journey north.

'Do you really think the goat will be saved?' asked
Snowy.

'Och, aye, laddie,' said the policeman. 'I ken Mr
MacAdam well. He's a gud vet, he'll save the wee
goatee if any man can.'

Snowy relaxed and sat back in the comfortable
back seat. So their efforts had not been in vain after all.

The policeman took off his cap and scratched his
head. He twisted round to face the Cubs.

'Tell me, noo,' he said. 'There's a wee thing that's
been bothering me. Did ye no come all this way tae
nicht in the back of that open truck, dressed as ye
are, in your thin jerseys?'

'Yes,' said Snowy. 'We wrapped our anoraks round
the goat.'

'On a bitterly cold nicht, like tae-nicht? Wha'
laddie, why did ye no' freeze to death?'

'Oh, we practised a few yoga asanas, the Shrimp,
Locust, Crab . . .'

'Stork, Greek Vase,' butted in Nobby. 'We even
Saluted the Sun.'

'It helps to improve the blood circulation and breathing system, and develops a healthy body and a healthy mind.'

The policeman grunted and turned to his driving partner.

'I've been around noo for twenty-five years, Jock,' he said, 'but ... but if I live tae be a hundred, I never will understand the crazy English.'

5 · The cold hand of Etchell

THE village of Billington lay white and silent. No cars or buses used the roads. Occasionally a pedestrian would trudge on, with hands in pockets and head down, anxious to be home behind securely fastened doors and windows. Even inside the cosy Group Headquarters, on that Friday evening, the atmosphere chilled the bones of the thirty Cubs who had braved the weather to attend their weekly Cub meeting. Snowflakes descended from the still darkness to carpet the land with white. Akela burst through the doorway in a flurry of snowflakes, carrying a bucket of snow. He slammed the door to to keep in the warm air, and strode to the top of the hall where he tipped his bucket of snow upside down on the tiled floor. He rubbed his frozen hands.

'Brrr, it's cold outside.'

He shivered. His Cubs shivered in sympathy. When he had warmed up sufficiently, he lifted up the bucket to leave a pile of snow on the floor tiles.

'Goo, can we have a snowball fight?' asked little Nobby.

'Shut up, war-monger,' said Akela.

Akela rubbed his hands again. 'Gather round, I'll show you how to make something,' he said. 'I'll show you how to make an igloo.'

'What's an igloo?' asked Nobby.

'An igloo is a house built of snow,' said Akela, squatting down before his pile of snow. 'It's used by Eskimos. Believe it or not, the inside of an igloo can be quite warm, so I'm told. Sometimes we have plenty of deep snow in England at this time of year, so it can be useful to know how the Eskimos build their igloos. I won't show you how to build a full-size igloo tonight, but gather round in a circle and I'll show you how to build a scale model igloo.'

'Whoopee!'

The Cubs squatted in a circle so they could all see Akela's demonstration.

'What you need to make a real, full-size igloo is a spade,' went on Akela, taking a steel rule from his pocket, 'but I'll use this instead.'

He patted the snow pile to make it smooth and well-packed, then with his rule, he cut out little snow blocks. Using these as building blocks, he built a circular wall on the floor about thirty centimetres in diameter.

'Notice the tops of the snow blocks slope down

towards the centre of the igloo,' he said, adding a second layer of blocks. 'Snow sticks to snow, so there is no need to use cement.'

Akela proceeded to add block after block until he had made a half sphere, the size of half a football.

'Now comes the clever bit,' said Akela.

He knelt down on the floor and carefully he cut a little doorway in his model igloo. On the opposite side, he cut another hole, somewhat smaller, half-way up the wall. For the window, he fitted a pane of ice, held in by packed snow. Around the door he built an entrance tunnel of snow blocks.

'And that's how to make an igloo,' he said. 'Come up one at a time and look at it closer, if you wish.'

The Cubs formed a line and came up one by one to examine the model igloo in detail.

'Six or seven years ago, a couple of Rover Scouts were caught in a blizzard on the Yorkshire Moors,'

went on Akela. 'One of the Rovers unfortunately twisted his knee and could not go on. The other saved his companion by building an igloo to shelter him, then he went off to fetch help. When you go to bed tonight, imagine what would have happened to those Rovers, had they not been able to build an igloo.'

Nobby stroked the model igloo like a pet tortoise. 'It's cold,' he said.

'You'd be cold if you were made of snow,' said Akela. He put the shovel under the igloo. 'Has everyone seen it?' he said.

There were no last cries of no. Akela scooped up the igloo on the shovel and dropped it in the bucket. The floor tiles were wet where a little of the snow had melted, but Akela soon showed his Cubs how to mop it up with a floor cloth.

'One word of warning,' went on Akela. 'Don't do at home on your mother's best carpet, what I've just done here on the tiles, or you'll be locked out for the night.' Akela sat on his chair. 'Talking about being locked out reminds me of a story . . .'

Shivers of curiosity and excitement made the Cubs' skins creep. They huddled in a circle to hear Akela's story.

'In the fourteen hundreds, there was a castle not far from here in Etchell's Woods. The place is nothing more than a ruin now, but in those days it was a

stout dwelling. It even had a dungeon. Now Earl
Etchell was a man with a violent temper. He imprisoned, in his dungeon, anyone who got in his way. One
man was imprisoned for twenty years for turning his
back on the earl as he passed. That the man did not
see him was no excuse. Another man was imprisoned
for ten years for getting in the way of the earl's
horse and carriage. That the man walked on crutches
and could not get out of the way in time, was no
excuse either. At one time, more than half of the men
on this vast estate were in the dungeon, so that the
earl had to force their women and children to work
in the fields for him.

'The dungeons were so overcrowded, there was
hardly room for the men to lie down. The food, what
little there was, was worse than that served to the
earl's dogs. The dungeon was stifling hot in summer
and icy cold in winter. Anyway, one cold January
night, like tonight, the prisoners broke out of the
dungeon and rounded up the castle staff, including
Earl Etchell. It was a bitterly cold night, and the
escaped prisoners turned the earl out of his castle.

'In those days, these parts were wooded for miles
around, and the earl could find no shelter from the
cold. He tried to claw his way, with his bare hands,
into the castle, through the thick, stone walls. What
finally happened to him, no one knows, but they say
his ghost still haunts Etchell's Castle even today.

His moans and scratching can still be heard on a cold January night in the ruins of the castle.

Nobby gulped. 'I'm . . . I'm not going anywhere near Et . . . Etchell's Castle again,' he said.

'What a pity, Nobby,' said Akela, 'for I am arranging to take the Pack out to Etchell's Castle tomorrow. There I shall give a demonstration of how to build a real, full-size igloo. We will go sledging down Etchell's Hill, and we will camp out in the snow, and have hot tea and sizzling sausages.'

Nobby's mouth watered. 'I'm not really scared of a silly old ghost,' he said. 'I bet the ghost won't come when our Pack is there, and if he did, we could chase him away by throwing snowballs at him. I like sausages and sledging.'

'Very well, very well. All those who want to go on tomorrow's winter outing must be here at ten o'clock in the morning, dressed in Cub uniform, with thick woollen socks and Wellington boots, warm anoraks and gloves. Any questions? No? Good!'

The next morning, Akela took his Cubs as far as he could in the Scout mini-bus. Driving conditions, however, were very bad, and Akela wisely parked the mini-bus before the narrow country lane reached the wooded range of hills. He loaded a borrowed sledge with groundsheets, blankets, tools and camping gear, and securely locked the mini-bus. Then, with a dozen Cubs hauling the sledge like Huskie dogs, the party set off up the wooded slopes to the ruins of Etchell's Castle.

The ruins were gaunt, desolate and uninviting, in spite of the scenic beauty of the surrounding landscape. Only one set of footprints, as far as Snowy could see, marked the white slope in front of the castle. The Cub Pack trudged through the ruined arch of the castle into the forecourt, where the snow showed not the slightest sign of being disturbed by man or beast. It seemed a pity to spoil it by walking on it.

A deep snow drift was banked along two walls. It was so deep it could have buried any one of the Cubs standing up, but this was just what Akela wanted to build his igloo. He beat the snow down with the back of his spade. Then he cut the blocks out of the well packed snow. Each and every Cub helped to build the igloo, which gradually took shape until it was the full-size version of the model Akela had built for them the previous night.

Next, Akela got his Cubs to spread the ground-sheets on the floor of the igloo, and on these they laid their blankets. The centre of the floor, however, they left clear for their cooker – a bottled-gas stove.

The igloo was only large enough to house six Cubs and Akela, so Akela supervised the cooking for each Six in rotation. The other Cubs, not cooking, were allowed to go sledging on the slope outside the castle. Each Six in turn, cooked the sausages, buttered the rolls and made the tea. Indeed, as Akela had said, an igloo could be quite cosy and comfortable.

As for the sledging, the site chosen by Akela could not have been better. When it was Snowy's turn to sledge, the slope had been run in by a hundred sledge rides. The snow was compressed and smooth. The sledge slipped so smoothly that it was a sensation almost like falling, until the sledge was gently pulled up in a low snow drift at the bottom of the slope. Then the sledge would be hauled up by hand to the top of the slope so another pair could have a ride.

Between rides, Snowy amused himself by admiring the scenery of the landscape spread out before him. It was, by far, the most beautiful landscape he had ever seen. He noticed again, the line of footprints which crossed the sledge run, and spiralled up the hill to the castle. It was a mystery who could have made these footprints at such an early hour. They were the footprints of a man, a big man, who staggered as he walked. Snowy frowned.

'Let's follow these tracks,' he suggested to Nobby, as they were waiting.

'Good idea, Snowy. I like tracking.'

The tracks were easy to follow. They spiralled up the slope to the side of the castle, but they stopped abruptly against a solid stone wall.

'He ... he's gone straight through the wall,' croaked Nobby.

'Or gone over it,' said Snowy, doubtfully.

He could not imagine why anyone would want to go over that wall three metres high. There was no sign that the footprints had been retraced.

By now, all thoughts of returning to the slope for their turn on the sledge had gone from Snowy's mind.

'He's ... he's gone straight through the wall,' repeated Nobby.

'Let's ... let's walk around the castle wall,' suggested Snowy.

'We . . . we might pick up the tracks again.'

Snowy led the way around the castle walls, with Nobby anxiously following him.

'Do you think . . . think they are the footprints of the ghost?' whimpered Nobby.

'What ghost?' said Snowy, trying to sound calm.

'The ghost of Earl Etchell, the ghost that scratches walls.'

'Oh, no, no,' said Snowy. 'It . . . it can't be.'

But to be honest, Snowy had not the faintest idea who, or what, could have made the footprints. Snowy and Nobby went all the way round the outside of the castle, and found no further tracks of any kind. They checked again inside the ruined grounds, particularly on the other side of the wall, but they saw no footprints there either. Snowy could see no one on the wall.

'It's the ghost, all right! I'm sure it's the ghost,' moaned Nobby. 'The footsteps go up to the other side of the castle wall and . . . and just disappear!'

A cold shiver went down Snowy's spine. He could think of no human explanation of the mystery.

By this time, the last six Cubs had finished their meals, and Akela showed them how to tidy up all the kit.

'One more sledge ride for everyone, a ten-minute snowball fight, then back to the mini-bus,' said Akela.

'We . . . we've found some footprints in the snow which lead nowhere,' Snowy said to Akela.

'Yeah, they came up the hill, round the side of the castle and through the stone wall,' said Nobby. 'It's . . . it's the wicked earl trying to scratch his way back into his castle.'

'What are you talking about?' said Akela in disbelief.

'We'll . . . we'll show you.'

Snowy led the way outside, and pointed to the tracks leading up to the stout wall. Now Akela was mystified. He looked all around the castle walls without picking up any further tracks. He prowled around inside the castle, now every bit as bewildered as Snowy.

'You're right,' he said. 'The footprints disappear into thin air.'

With Nobby still clutching the back of his anorak, Snowy entered the remains of the great hall, now open to the sky. At the far end of the great hall was a huge open fire-place, large enough to swallow half-a-dozen men, but now half buried in a snowdrift. Snowy looked up inside the chimney, but he could see nothing but blackness. Nobby looked inside. They heard a whimpering moan and a scratching noise.

'It's . . . it's the ghost!' said Nobby. 'Let's get out of here.'

'Ssh!' said Snowy.

The moaning and rustling stopped. There was now a deathly silence. Snowy poked his head into the chimney again. Nobby also had a little peep.

Suddenly a cold, bony hand shot out and grabbed Snowy by the throat. Nobby screamed. Instinctively, Snowy grabbed the clutching wrist and pulled. A cry echoed within the chimney and a big, bony frame of a man fell on top of the two Cubs. Nobby screeched and scampered away to safety. Snowy stood back and faced the man he had pulled down into the snowdrift.

'Why don't you get lost!' growled the man, pulling himself out of the snowdrift.

He was tall and ragged. He had thick hair and a black beard, but his skin was chalk white, blue in parts around his lips and the back of his hands with the cold. His well-worn blue serge suit was quite inadequate to keep him warm.

'I didn't expect to find anyone in the chimney,' explained Snowy.

Just then Akela came striding up, with Nobby at his heels.

'It's the ghost, it's the ghost,' shrieked Nobby. 'Look, there he is, talking to Snowy.'

'Now what's going on here,' said Akela, in a voice which made him sound like a policeman.

'Why don't you keep your kids away from here,' growled the man, rubbing his bony hands and stamping his feet.

'My Cubs have a perfect right to be here,' said Akela. 'We are camping out and there's no law against that.'

At the words 'camping out', the man smiled faintly for the first time.

'I used to do a lot of camping when I was young,' he said. He scowled again. 'But you've no right to come bothering me.'

The man turned to go back into the chimney.

'Haven't you got anywhere better than that to stay?' asked Akela.

'You've got to have a job to afford to live in a

house,' said the man over his shoulder, 'and you've got to have an address before you can get a job.'

'But can't you live in a hostel for a while?'

'With a lot of down and outs like me?' snarled the man, angrily. 'Look, mister, if I can't stand on my own two feet, I prefer not to stand at all.'

'I was trying to help,' said Akela.

The man turned on Akela. 'What do you know?' he said. 'What do you know? I used to be well off like you, with a house and job, then I broke my leg and lost my job. I had to take to thieving to make ends meet, then I got put in prison. My wife died and my house was sold up, so when I came out of prison, I had nothing.'

'But there must be some . . .' began Akela.

'Ah, nobody wants to know an ex-jailbird, believe me. They hate me as much as I hate myself, and I can't stand the sight of myself, or the sound of my own name. So clear off and leave me alone.'

The man climbed back into the shelter of the chimney. Akela shrugged his shoulders and walked away.

'Can't . . . can't we help him?' asked Snowy. 'He'll freeze to death up there.'

'You heard what he said,' said Akela. 'He doesn't want any help. He wants to stand on his own two feet. There are a lot of people like that, especially the old folk.'

'But we can't let him freeze to death.'

Akela stopped before the pile of camping kit. He picked up a few items and took them to the open fireplace.

'You can borrow some of our camping kit if you like,' he shouted up the chimney.

The only reply he got was a disagreeable grunt.

Akela left a couple of groundsheets and a pile of blankets, the bottled-gas stove, pots, pans and cutlery. The Cubs had scoffed all the sausages, but there was a bit of tea, milk, bread, cheese and cooking fat left. Akela left all these items in the mouth of the fireplace.

'Send them back to us when you've finished,' shouted Akela up the chimney. 'We're the 2nd Billington Cub Scout Pack.'

Akela walked away without waiting for an answer. Snowy did not expect to see that camping kit again, but Akela did not let him have the time to ponder about that. He made sure that everyone had a last ride on the sledge down the slope. He organised a ten-minute snowball fight to warm up his Cubs. Then they left for their long trek back to the mini-bus, dragging with them their sledge, and what was left of their camping kit.

Two weeks later, the Cubs turned up for their Friday evening Cub meeting, expecting to take their tests for badges. That programme was cancelled. Before Akela stood a brand new hamper.

'The old man we helped at Etchell's Castle has returned our camping kit,' said Akela, opening the lid of the hamper. 'As you can see, the kit has been properly cleaned and polished and the gas bottle replaced with a full bottle. In addition, there is a load of food, sausages, eggs, bacon, bread, tea, cakes and so on, so instead of having our badge tests this evening, we'll have a party.'

The Cubs cheered. They organised a party in the cosy confines of the Cub hall.

'I wonder what happened to that man?' asked Snowy.

'I knew he wasn't a ghost,' said Nobby, munching at a hot sausage. 'Those footprints we tracked were too well made. They were definitely human. I knew all the time.'

'I've found a letter,' said Akela, pulling a folded paper from the bottom of the hamper. He opened the notepaper.

'Dear friends,' he read out. 'Thank you for lending me your camping gear which I return. I spent the night in your igloo, and had the best night's sleep I've had since my accident six and a half years ago. It certainly helped to restore my self-respect. With best wishes for the future, signed John Etchell.'

'Etchell?' said Snowy. 'That's . . . that's the name of the ghost!'

'As soon as I saw him I knew he was a ghost,' said

Nobby. 'I'm not going to Etchell's Castle again, that's for sure.'

'He can't be a ghost,' said Snowy, 'and yet . . . and yet it's too much of a coincidence that his name is Etchell. Perhaps he changed his name. He said he couldn't stand the sound of his own name, and since he was in Etchell's Castle at the time, Etchell seems the most likely name he would think of.'

'That is the most likely explanation,' agreed Akela. He smiled faintly. 'But the truth is, we can never be really sure if he was a ghost or not.'

All this talk put the Cubs off their food. They sat around in a chilled stupor, except Nobby.

'Well, ghost or not,' he said, helping himself to another sausage, 'his sausages are real.'

6 · Run to ground

THE 2nd Billington strikers in white shirts came down the field. The ball swung from one wing to another, leaving the defenders in red shirts confused. The winger added to the defenders' bewilderment by sending across the goalmouth, a low, wicked, curving centre. Snowy volleyed the ball goalwards. The ball zipped low along the ground for the corner of the net. Nobby, the opposing goalkeeper in this practice match, scrambled along the goal-line, but he had to stretch himself to reach the ball and tip it round the goalpost.

Akela blew his whistle.

'Very good, very good,' he said. 'Your ball control is good, your tactics are good, in fact on the whole your play is very good. But you still don't go after the ball as fast as you ought to. You should be able to run much faster than you do. Next week, instead of our usual practice football match, I want to take you on a cross-country run to St Giles' Abbey and back.'

'That's a long way,' said Nobby.

'It's not far, only a couple of kilometres along the public footpath. Now, where were we?' Akela kicked the ball to the corner flag. 'Corner to whites. Mark your men, reds.'

The practice match proceeded in deadly earnest for a further hour. Snowy trudged off the field, well pleased with their progress, but he knew Akela was right about their play. The 2nd Billingtons could play football well enough. After all, it was February now, and the Cubs had been playing together every week since the beginning of the football season. But they were still a little slow going after the ball.

'Are you running next week, Nobby?' asked Snowy, pulling off his white football shirt.

'Sure!' said Nobby. 'I like running, 'cept when somebody's after me.'

'Let's go on a little practice run tomorrow. I haven't run a couple of kilometres before, and I want to see if I can do it.'

'Good idea, Snowy. Give me a call when you're ready.'

'O.K., Nobby.'

The next morning, Snowy and Nobby set out for a practice run to St Giles' Abbey. The country track was twisty, with sudden rises and dips, yet Nobby set off at a cracking pace. About a hundred metres later, he was gasping and panting like a weary old carthorse. Snowy then took the lead. His legs were heavy and it was an effort to put one foot in front of the other. Snowy puffed like a little steam engine, and found he could keep going.

Snowy kept going with Nobby gasping like a goldfish behind him. They struggled on at no more than a trot, until they almost reached St Giles' Abbey. They had only a hundred metres to go when the path turned into a hairpin bend to by-pass a plot of land which was used for building. Snowy followed the path. Nobby took a short cut across the building plot. That was a mistake.

Snowy saw Nobby take the short cut, and increased his speed around the bend to cut down Nobby's lead. He turned the bend to come back on the other side of the building plot just as Nobby let out a yell. For a moment Nobby hopped around, then he sat on a pile of wet sand.

'I've got a pebble in my shoe,' he said.

Snowy waited while Nobby pulled off his shoe to shake the pebble out. Just as Nobby put on his shoe again, the builder appeared behind him. He was a giant of a man, built like a gorilla.

'Ah, caught you,' he said, making a grab for Nobby.

Nobby yelped and jumped away before the builder could catch him. The builder turned on Snowy.

'There's been a lot of stealing around here . . .'

Snowy stood his ground. 'We haven't stolen anything.'

The builder towered over Snowy. Snowy stood up to him.

'We did not steal anything,' repeated Snowy. 'We're Cubs . . .'

The builder bent over Snowy. 'I've lost over a hundred pounds worth of materials since I started on this plot, and it's got to stop. Now get off with you before I call the police. If I catch you around here stealing again, I'll put you in the cement-mixer!'

'I tell you we did not steal any of your materials and you should make sure of your facts before you start blaming anyone . . .'

'I know your sort,' snorted the builder. 'You'd steal anything the minute I turn my back. Now get off with you before . . .'

'Snowy, Snowy,' called Nobby from the footpath. 'Let's go, Snowy. It looks like rain, and I don't want to end up in the cement-mixer.'

Snowy almost choked with anger, but he knew he was wasting his time arguing with this man. He walked across to Nobby.

'Don't let me see you round these parts again,' shouted the builder. 'I won't be so lenient with you next time I find your hanging about here.'

Snowy had committed no crime. He always respected other people's property, and he found it hard to be unfairly blamed for stealing, of all things. He walked along the path with Nobby, but he dis-

liked having to go away without having proved their
innocence. He could not understand why the builder
had been so keen to accuse them of a crime they had
not committed.

Snowy was in two minds as to whether to forget
the whole unpleasant experience, or whether to go
back and sort it out once and for all. Clearly the man
had no right to accuse the Cubs of stealing without
evidence. He should be stopped before he made false
accusations against others.

'Just a minute, Nobby,' said Snowy, stopping by
an old oak tree. The impulse to look back was
irresistible. 'I'd like to see just why he wanted to get
rid of us so quickly.'

Snowy climbed up the oak so he could see back to
the building plot beside St Giles' Abbey. He watched
the builder patrol the plot, checking on the materials
which were stacked around. All was quiet, apart from
the Abbey clock which struck twelve. The builder
climbed into his van.

Snowy shrugged his shoulders and started to climb
down the tree again, but he had to wait as Nobby
was climbing up.

'Steady on, Snowy, you're sitting on my head,' said
Nobby, coming up too fast.

Snowy moved aside on to another bough to let
Nobby come up beside him. He looked back at the
building plot and was surprised to see the builder's

van, instead of driving off, had reversed back to the newly built house. The builder got out and opened the van rear doors. He had a good look round then he stealthily slipped into the new house. He re-appeared three separate times, carrying a coil of electrical cable, a few strips of wood, and a sink unit top, which he slid into the back of his van. The complete loading operation was over in two minutes. The van drove away, and once more the area was as quiet as the Abbey grave-yard.

'Did you see that?' asked Snowy.

'See what?' said Nobby.

'The builder took a sink unit top, a coil of cable and lengths of new timber from the new house, and drove off with it.'

Snowy could not see why new materials should be taken out of a new house.

'What's wrong with that?' said Nobby.

'He's ... he's stealing his own materials. People don't take new materials *from* a new house, do they?'

'Oh, I see what you mean,' said Nobby.

'And he's trying to put the blame on us!'

'The rotten old faker,' said Nobby. 'But we can't stop him stealing his own stuff, can we?'

'N ... no, I suppose not.'

Nobby climbed down the tree.

'I'll race you back to Group Headquarters. Come on, Snowy, it looks like rain.'

The Cubs ran back along the path. Snowy could not understand the odd behaviour of the builder. After running about three hundred metres, Snowy again settled down to the rhythm of a long-distance runner. This left his mind free to think about the builder.

Was the builder really stealing his own building materials? If so why? To sell again? Snowy could not quite work it out. He was still angry that the builder had accused him of stealing. Snowy wanted to do something to put the matter straight, but he did not know what to do.

The practice run was a success in as much as it proved to the Cubs how little they knew about cross-country running. They arrived back at their starting point, hardly able to stand on their own feet.

Next week twenty Cub Scouts gathered at their Group Headquarters for the same cross-country run. Snowy told Akela of their practice run the previous week, and of their strange encounter with the builder.

'You'll find you can run much easier today, as your training run will have loosened up your muscles,' said Akela. Akela scratched his head. 'As for the builder, I can't see what I can do about that.'

Snowy shrugged his shoulders. He thought the best thing he could do now was to put the whole matter completely out of his head.

Snowy and Nobby had fully recovered from the stresses and strains of their practice run and were anxious to get on their way. From the start, they took the lead. Snowy soon settled down to the steady rhythm of a runner. He felt he could run on all day. Akela was right. The practice run last week had, as Akela had said, successfully shaken the stiffness out of his body.

Snowy set such a cracking pace that only Nobby could keep up. The other Cubs in the Pack dropped steadily behind, but Snowy did not slacken up. He ran like the wind. His strides were long and graceful, his breathing smooth and powerful. To run like this was almost like flying.

Nobby kept in the running by sheer stamina and grim determination, but when they came up to the hairpin bend leading to the Abbey, he took the short cut across the building plot. Snowy saw exactly what happened as he came round the other side of the bend. Nobby ran straight between the builder and a policeman.

'That's one of them,' shrieked the builder, pointing after Nobby'

'Hey, you boy,' said the policeman.

Nobby looked back over his shoulder. The policeman beckoned.

'Come here, boy,' he said calmly.

Nobby looked around.

'Who me?' he said.

'Yes, you. I'd like a word with you.'

'There's another one,' yelled the builder, as Snowy
ran up to see what was going on. 'These two were

hanging around here just before the materials were stolen. I warned them at the time. I told them to keep away.'

'You're not saying these boys stole your materials, are you?' said the policeman in surprise.

'I've got no proof, but I've got my suspicions . . .'

'They couldn't carry the stuff for a start!'

'Oh, well, er, maybe not. But they could have been spying out the land for the bigger boys. Well, I don't know who stole all my stuff, but somebody did, and I have to charge extra for my buildings to cover these losses.'

The policeman turned to the Cubs.

'And what have you to say to that?' said the policeman.

'We didn't steal anything,' said Snowy. 'We are Cubs on a cross-country run . . .'

Just then Akela came running up with the main body of his Cubs.

'Hullo, hullo, hullo,' said Akela, sounding like a policeman himself. 'What's going on here?'

'This big gorilla is accusing us of stealing his things again,' said Nobby.

'Oh?' said Akela.

'I didn't say that exactly,' said the builder, 'but somebody is stealing my materials. Last weekend somebody stole a sink unit top from this new house . . .'

'I know who stole your sink unit top,' said Nobby.

'Oh, who?' grunted the builder in disbelief.

'You!' said Akela. 'And the timber and cable and other things, and you tried to put the blame on my Cubs.'

The builder turned as red as a beetroot.

'Ah, er . . .' he stuttered. 'It seems this conversation is getting out of hand . . . Maybe I did make a mistake about you . . . Let's forget about the whole affair, shall we, eh?'

The builder must have suddenly felt weak at the knees, for he groped backwards for a nearby pile of bricks and sat down. He pulled out a handkerchief and mopped his bald head. But the policeman hadn't finished with him.

'I don't think we should forget about it yet,' he said gruffly. 'It seems to me that you stole your own materials, to give you an excuse to put up your building charges to cover your "losses". And to take the suspicion off yourself, you blame anyone who comes along. These are serious charges.'

'Well, er, yes, no, I mean, not exactly . . . Let's forget the whole affair, shall we?'

'You'd better come along with me to the police station to make a statement. I'll get a warrant to search your home and garage. I expect we'll soon be able to tell you exactly who stole your material.'

'Oh, no, no no no, that won't be necessary. I . . . I'll confess. Er, I only did it as a joke . . .'

The policeman took the builder and led him to a waiting police car. The Cubs watched them drive away.

'I don't think that thieving builder will try that trick again in a hurry,' said Akela. 'Now, where were we? Oh, this run. Hey, Snowy, if you can run on the football field as fast as you ran away from me today, you'll put the wind up the goalie.'

Nobby sat on the pile of bricks and mopped his forehead with his handkerchief.

'Not half as much as we put the wind up that great, big, thieving gorilla,' he said.

7 · Match of the season

THE nights grew lighter and the weather warmer as March arrived. The winter season had almost passed. As Akela had forecast, his Cubs had enjoyed their winter outings. They had played many sports, such as football, walking, swimming, boating, yoga, sledging and running, but of all their winter sports, they liked football best. They practised every week, and it is quite true to say, they played better every time they practised.

'Can you arrange another game with West Park?' Snowy asked Akela.

'At football,' butted in Nobby.

Akela scratched his head. 'West Park have a full fixture list. Their instructor said he would let me know when they can give us a game. They have been booked up for weeks now, but when the nights become a little lighter, we'll give them an evening game. Incidentally, did you know Stanley Town have reached the semi-final of the All-England Football Cup? I saw it in the newspaper last night. They are playing off their semi-final at Stretford Park reserve ground next week against a team either from Derby or London.'

'May we go to see them?' asked Snowy. 'I'd like to see Chunky Craig and his team again.'

'Yes, yes, so would I,' mused Akela. 'I'll see what I can do.'

'We can give them a game if we don't play West Park,' said Nobby.

'Shut up, trouble-maker,' said Akela. 'We will never play them, they're too good for us, but we can watch them.'

There was a big match fever at Stretford Park reserve ground on the Saturday of the semi-finals. The turnstiles clicked continuously as spectators from two counties came to see their teams. Although the Cubs arrived forty-five minutes before the kick-off, the terraces were already filling up. Programme sellers and hot-dog vendors did a roaring trade. Akela ushered his Pack down the terrace to the front, near the players' tunnel, so he could keep an eye on them in a group. A band of Scottish pipes and drums kept the crowds amused before the teams turned out.

Ten minutes before kick-off, a team of London boys ran on to the pitch clad in the Arsenal colours, red and white. But the greater cheer greeted the local Lancashire lads when they trooped out in their purple and blue shirts.

The teams went to their respective goals to loosen up with a kick about before the game started. It was apparent that this was going to be the match of the day. The weather was fine with no wind. The ground was dry and the turf newly mown. The players in both goal-mouths flicked the balls about with uncanny accuracy and ease. They were in a class by themselves. They knew how to play football at its best.

'We are the champions!' shouted Nobby, clapping his hands.

'Who are we?' asked Akela.

'The 2nd Billington Cubs,' said Nobby, turning around.

Akela groaned and turned Nobby's head round to face the football pitch.

Stanley Town kicked off. It was clear that the manoeuvres were pre-planned. Attacking movements, from both sides, first one then the other, proceeded like clockwork. More than that, each player had his own special skill.

Snowy's hero, and the player of the match, was Chunky Craig, who played as a striker. It was Chunky who scored the most spectacular and probably the cheekiest goal Snowy had ever seen. In the goal-mouth scramble, several players, including Chunky, were lying on the ground. Chunky picked up the ball with his feet, and flung it over his head into the empty goal net. Stanley Town were one up.

There was no further score. The one–nil victory for the Stanley Town boys meant they had reached the final of the All-England Junior Football Cup. Crowds leapt on the field to surround the players.

'You Cubs stay where you are so I can keep an eye on you until the crowds thin out,' said Akela, firmly.

Not that any of the Cubs wanted to move away just yet. Eventually the Stanley Town boys made their way to the players' entrance.

'Congratulations, Chunky,' said Snowy, as Chunky passed, almost within reach. 'Best of luck in the final.'

Chunky looked up. 'Hi, Snowy,' he said. 'How are you?'

'It was a great match.'

'Thanks. How is your football going?'

'We play on most days, whenever we can.'

'Great! How about a game some time?'

Snowy shrugged his shoulders. 'Oh, we are not in your class.'

'Yes we are,' said Nobby.

'It doesn't matter, it's only a game,' said Chunky. 'Our players are still keen to take you on, to make up for our last defeat. Are you playing anyone next Saturday?'

'No, but . . .'

'Good. We are free then. How about it?'

'Well . . .'

Chunky was ushered on by the crowds.

'We'll leave it to the trainers to fix up, eh? See you . . . 'bye!'

''Bye!' said Snowy. He frowned. He wondered what he had let himself in for.

Once the players had left the field, the crowds quickly thinned out.

'We'll move off now for a mug of tea at the mini-bus,' said Akela. 'Keep together. I don't want to lose any of you now.'

The Cubs went on to their mini-bus. Akela brewed up the tea to give the traffic time to clear.

'Akela!' said Snowy. 'I had a word with Chunky

Craig, the Stanley Town captain. He wants us to give him a game next Saturday.'

Akela spluttered.

'Don't talk like that when I'm drinking tea,' he coughed. 'What are you trying to do, choke me? Huh, you must be joking. Stanley Town can play any team in the country. Why pick on us?'

'Because we beat them at cricket, I suppose.'

'And they want to get a cricket score against us, eh? No, thanks, definitely not, and that's final. Now don't mention it again. I want to drink my tea without choking myself to death.'

Snowy shrugged his shoulders. Akela was right of course. It was sporting of Chunky to offer them a game. Perhaps he was only being polite. There would be no match between Stanley Town and the 2nd Billington Cubs. It was sad in a way, but it was also a great relief. As far as Stanley Town was concerned, the Billington Cubs would be merely spectators to the football wizards.

But at their next Cub meeting, Akela was clearly in a state of anxiety.

'I had a phone-call from the Stanley Town trainer,' he said breathlessly. 'He wants us to give his lads a game at South Lancs Playing Fields on Saturday!'

'Good-oh!' said Nobby.

'What . . . what did you tell him?' asked Snowy.

'I . . . I said yes! I said no at first, but he was

insistent. He said he just wanted his lads to have a gentle little practice game before their big match, their cup final, the following week. He wants his lads to polish up their tactics!'

Snowy groaned. 'Book of Records, here we come,' he thought.

'He wants to use us as sparring partners!' croaked Akela.

'We'll use them as our sparring partners,' said Nobby, prancing about like a boxer.

'Oh dear, oh dear, oh dear!' said Akela, turning away. 'Ignorance is bliss. Oh dear, oh dear, oh dear!'

To match Akela's spirits, it rained very heavily during the night before the match, but it was fine in the morning so the game was not cancelled. The Cubs met again at Group Headquarters. They collected their kit, piled into the mini-bus and drove off for their match at South Lancs Playing Fields.

Akela had timed the journey so they would have no spare time for nervousness before the match. They arrived ten minutes before the pre-arranged kick-off time, just time to change before the game. The Stanley Town bus had arrived before them, but only ten of their players had turned up. Neither Chunky, their skipper, nor their star goalkeeper, Chris Sharples, or even their trainer was there.

'They got off the coach in Manchester to pick up

some fruit juice,' said Mike Jones, their vice-captain. 'The bus-driver wouldn't wait for them.'

Akela grunted. 'We'll wait.' He turned to his Cubs. 'Get changed now. You can have a little kick about for a few minutes.'

Both teams changed. Snowy led his team to one of the goals to limber up. Last Saturday at this time, he had seen the Stanley Town boys flick the ball about at Stretford reserve ground as if it was a balloon. To Snowy, and to the rest of his team, the ball was as heavy as lead.

The missing Stanley Town players had not turned up five minutes after the official kick-off time. It looked like rain so it was decided to start the game without them. Stanley Town only fielded ten players, but they were strong enough to whack the Cubs with half that number.

As Snowy ran up the field for the toss-up, he noticed that the Stanley Town players in the other goal-mouth were not flicking the ball around with their usual skill and zest. He noted that they, too, found the ball heavy and the ground sticky.

Snowy won the toss and decided to play with the wind. If only his side could score an early goal, and then play like tigers to hold on to the lead, the Cubs would win. In spite of the odds against them, the Cubs lined up for the kick-off.

'Don't try anything fancy,' Snowy told his team

mates. 'Keep the ball low and stick to short passing.'

Stanley Town kicked off with a team of ten re-shuffled players. To make matters worse for them, the heavy ground did not suit their style of play.

The tactics of the Billington Cubs, on the other hand, were just right. Their many hours of practising in the muddy fields behind Group Headquarters had given them just the training they needed for this game.

The result was that Stanley Town did not have things all their own way. As one Stanley Town player said afterwards, 'I never got the ball without two red-shirted players being on top of me at the same time.'

The short passing tactics of the Billington Cubs were not spectacular, but they were the only means of gaining ground in such conditions. On one occasion, the Billington forward line progressed up the field to within two metres of the Stanley goal. Only then did Snowy try a shot. Walter Hains was a first class centre-back, but not so good as a stand-in goalkeeper. He was unable to reach the ball on the slippery ground, before it had trickled over the goal-line. The Cubs had scored. Akela blew his whsitle and danced with joy.

'Goal! Goal!' he screeched.

Billington 1, Stanley Town 0.

That goal cheered the hearts of the Billington Cubs. But Stanley was too good a team to be put off by that. They were soon on the attack. They attacked the goal from all directions. Nobby, the Billington goalkeeper, was black from head to toe in the muddy goal-mouth. Stanley forced a corner.

It was an exciting game. There was a spectator behind the goal, the Stanley Town coach-driver. Whilst the teams were taking up their positions for the corner kick, he put out a bony hand and touched Nobby on the shoulder.

'Pssst!' he said in a low voice.

Nobby turned. When he saw the grinning face near his, he nearly jumped out of his skin. He let out a yell and jumped in the arms of Akela. Akela was knocked off-balance on the slippery ground. He slithered and slipped, skidded and spun in a desperate effort to keep on his feet. Nobby, screeching at the top of his voice, grabbed Akela's waving leg. All this was too much for Akela. He lost his balance and sat in a puddle. Nobby fell on his head.

'Get off, get off, you dirty little menace,' yelled Akela, pushing Nobby away. 'You nearly made me swallow my whistle.'

'It's the ghost, it's the ghost,' said Nobby, climbing over Akela's chest.

'Ghost?' said the stranger, somewhat puzzled.

The man had shaved off his beard, but Snowy recognised him as John Etchell, the man they had helped two months ago at Etchell's castle.

'Remember me?' said the man. 'You let me borrow your camping kit when I was homeless and out of a job.'

Akela got up. 'Oh, I remember,' he said.

'Er . . . er, I don't want to hold up your game . . . just wish you the best of luck. I'll . . . I'll never forget how you helped me. I've got a job now, coach-driver, and I've got a nice little flat.'

'I'm very pleased to hear it,' grunted Akela.

Nobby plucked up his courage a little. He peered round Akela's leg.

'Hullo, ghost,' said Nobby. 'Have you got any more sausages?'

The man put up his hand to hide his mouth from the opposing team.

'As a matter of fact,' he whispered, 'I drove the

Lancashire lads here to play you this morning. Oh, the way they were bragging about beating you made me angry. I left two of them and their coach in Manchester.'

'Eh?' said Nobby, cocking his hand behind his ear. 'Speak up, will you, I can't hear you. Did you say you left two sausages in the coach in Manchester?'

'Ssh!' said the man.

'You mean you deliberately left them behind in Manchester?' said Akela, in a low voice. 'I mean the players, not the sausages.'

'Ssh!' said the man. 'I did it to help you.'

'That's no help to us,' said Akela in despair. 'These lads are our friends. They came a long way to give us a game . . . You would have done us a good turn if you had helped them and everybody else for that matter . . .' Akela breathed hard, but he must have known he was wasting his time. 'Ah, what's the use,' he said. He turned back to the players. 'Get ready for the corner,' he said, and blew his whistle.

'I'm . . . I'm sorry,' said the man. 'I was only trying to help. I'll . . . I'll make up to the lads when I drive them home tonight, honest I will . . .'

Billington survived that corner, in fact they held on to their one–nil lead until half-time. Then the Stanley trainer, very breathless, and his two star players turned up.

'Did you have any trouble getting here?' Snowy

asked Chunky, as they walked on the pitch for the second half.

'I'll say we did,' said Chunky. 'We stopped off at a shop to get something to drink and some sausage rolls, but the bus-driver wouldn't wait for us. We had to get a taxi. Now would you believe it, the taxi had a leaking radiator, and it took us an hour to get across Manchester.'

'Better late than never,' said Snowy.

The two substitutes in their clean purple and blue shirts were a remarkable contrast to their mud-stained companions. The teams lined up and kicked off.

At once Stanley, at full strength, forced the pace, determined to make up for lost time. The Billington Cubs were forced back into their own penalty area.

Although Billington had played very hard for their one-goal lead, Snowy felt uneasy. It was not the Cubs' fault, but Stanley Town had only played with ten players throughout the whole of the first half, and they had been without their two best players. Snowy did not want to win a game if his opponents were unfairly handicapped. When the ball came over for a centre, Snowy caught it in his hands.

'Penalty!' yelled many voices together.

The Stanley Town trainer, who was refereeing in the second half, blew his whistle.

'What's up with you?' said Louie, in surprise.

'I was just giving them a fair chance,' said Snowy.

Snowy walked away with his head down. He had thrown the game away, but at least he had given Stanley a fair chance to get even.

Chunky Craig, fresh and just warming-up to the game, was to take the penalty kick. But he had yet to learn that the ball was heavy and the ground slippery. The shot skidded towards the goal agonisingly slowly. Nobby in fact, dived the wrong way, but he was able to get up and scramble back along the goal-line like a little bunny to smother the ball.

Stanley had failed to score. They had been given a fair chance and failed, and now Snowy felt he could play to win with a clear conscience. He rallied his team.

'Away, Billington,' he yelled, booting the ball to the first in a line of red-shirted players.

Billington went away with the Stanley players slithering in the mud after them. Billington did not score again, the effort was too great for them, but neither did Stanley Town. The referee looked at his watch and blew his whistle for full time. Billington had won. Akela danced on the field.

'You've done it! You've done it!' he yelled at his Cubs. 'You've beaten the best junior football team in England. I knew you would, but I can't believe it.'

The Cubs found it difficult to believe either. They were still a little dazed in the mini-bus on their way home.

'What a magnificent ending to our winter sports' season,' said Akela, as he drove along the Queen's highway.

'Ending?' said Nobby. 'You mean . . . we are not going to have any more winter games?'

Snowy looked out of the window. Already the banks of the highway were covered in crowds of daffodils in full bloom. Akela noticed the blaze of colour too, as bright as sunshine.

'Our winter sports' season is over. But it's not really an ending.' Akela grinned. 'Let's say it's the start of our new summer season.'

THE WORST KIDS IN THE WORLD

Barbara Robinson

The six Herdmans were absolutely the worst kids in the history of the world. When they weren't setting fire to buildings they were clonking each other and terrorizing the other kids at the Woodrow Wilson School. This particular Christmas they decided to take over all the star parts in the Sunday school pageant, and everyone knew trouble was brewing.

'A wonderfully funny, very moving and utterly joyful book'
Children's Books of the Year

POEMS THAT GO BUMP IN THE NIGHT

Zenka and Ian Woodward

Are you afraid of ghosts?

Here is a blood-curdling collection of poems about the things that frighten us at night. Flapping curtains silhouetted against a full moon . . . coffin lids opening slowly . . . phantom horsemen galloping through inky black woods.

The safest place to read this book is tucked up under your bedcovers with a torch. Or is it *really* safe . . .

If you're an eager Beaver reader, perhaps you ought to try some more of our exciting titles. They are available in bookshops or they can be ordered directly from us. Just complete the form below and enclose the right amount of money and the books will be sent to you at home.

☐	THE SUMMER OF THE WAREHOUSE	Sally Bicknell	£1.25
☐	THE GOOSEBERRY	Joan Lingard	£1.25
☐	FOX CUB BOLD	Colin Dann	£1.50
☐	GHOSTLY AND GHASTLY	Barbara Ireson Ed.	£1.50
☐	WHITE FANG	Jack London	£1.25
☐	JESS AND THE RIVER KIDS	Judith O'Neill	£1.50
☐	A PATTERN OF ROSES	K. M. Peyton	£1.25
☐	YOU TWO	Jean Ure	£1.50
☐	SNOWY RIVER BRUMBY	Elyne Mitchell	£1.25

If you would like to hear more about Beaver Books, and discover all the latest news, don't forget the BEAVER BULLETIN. If you just send a stamped self-addressed envelope to Beaver Books, Brookmount House, 62-65 Chandos Place, Covent Garden, London WC2N 4NW, we will send you the latest BULLETIN.

If you would like to order books, please send this form, and the money due to:

HAMLYN PAPERBACK CASH SALES, PO BOX 11, FALMOUTH, CORNWALL, TR10 9EN.

Send a cheque or postal order, and don't forget to include postage at the following rates: UK: 55p for first book, 22p for second, 14p thereafter; BFPO and Eire: 55p for first book, 22p for second, 14p per copy for next 7 books, 8p per book thereafter; Overseas: £1.00 for first book, 25p thereafter.

NAME ....

ADDRESS ....

....

Please print clearly

If you're an eager Beaver reader, perhaps you ought to try some more of our exciting titles. They are available in bookshops or they can be ordered directly from us. Just complete the form below and enclose the right amount of money and the books will be sent to you at home.

And if you would like to hear more about Beaver Books, and find out all the latest news, don't forget the Beaver Bulletin. If you just send a stamped-addressed envelope to Beaver Books, Brookmount House, 62-65 Chandos Place, Covent Garden, London WC2N 4NW, we will send you the latest one.

If you would like to order books, please send this form, and the money due to:

HAMLYN PAPERBACK CASH SALES, PO BOX 11, FALMOUTH, CORNWALL TR10 9EN.

Send a cheque or postal order, and don't forget to include postage at the following rates: UK: 55p for first book, 22p for second, 14p thereafter; BFPO and Eire: 55p for first book, 22p for second, 14p per copy for next 7 books, 8p per book thereafter; Overseas: £1.00 for first book, 25p thereafter.

NAME...

ADDRESS..

....

Please print clearly